3D Beading Patterns

Collection of 20-faced Ball Projects

APRIL DAYS

3D BEADING PATTERNS: COLLECTION OF 20-FACED BALL PROJECTS

Copyright © 2023 by April Days.

All rights reserved. No part of this book may be reproduced, distributed, or transmitted in any form or any means, including photocopying, recording, or other electronic or mechanical methods, without the prior written permission of the publisher, except in the case of brief quotations embodied in reviews and certain other non-commercial uses permitted by copyright law.

Publisher: Riverhorns Publishing

For information contact: Riverthathorn@gmail.com

Book and Cover design by April Days

ISBN: 978-1-7782740-9-1

First Edition: January 2023

TABLE OF CONTENT

Contents

Summer Garden 1
Country Breeze 11
Night Lure 21
Desert Green 31
Blue Magic 41
Singing Spring 51
Orange Dream 61
Hot Coral 71
Ice Reflection 81
Christmas Greeting 91

Preface

Play with Perler beads is fun. Can you make decorative 3D balls with Perler beads? Yes, you can! This book is a collection of ten pattern designs with instructions on how to make them using Perler beads. The finished crafts are the size of a soccer ball or a basketball, depending on the number of rows used. All the balls are made from 20 pieces of triangles which give the crafts a unique and artistic look.

With easy-to-follow design patterns, step-by-step instructions, and graphic illustrations, you use Perler beads to make various decorative balls on your own at home. These handmade crafts are durable and long-lasting.

Whether you are looking to add a touch of whimsy to your home décor or searching for the perfect gift, the Perler bead creations are sure to impress. The intricate patterns and vibrant color choices of the beads make for a stunning finished craft that is sure to be a conversation starter.

In addition to their decorative value, the Perler bead crafts are a great way to exercise your creative thinking and try new techniques. So why wait? Start exploring the world of Perler beads in a new way today and bring a little magic into your life.

Summer Garden

BALL DESCRIPTION:

15 rows, approximately the size of soccer ball, made with 20 pieces of triangles

MATERIALS

1. Perler Beads: 6,690 pieces, 9 colors
2. Ball Beads: 12 pieces, 12 mm in diameter, 1 color
3. Beading String: fishing line – 6 lbs. 145 in for one triangle piece and the ball bead
4. Inside filling: used plank foam

TOOLS

1. Needle: size of 2.5 in
2. Curved needle: size of 3.5 in
3. Scissors
4. Stainless steel tweezer

Color and Number of Beads

1) Perler beads:

Symbol ID	Color preview	Count
Y		900
R		2 160
P		660
O		1 020
M		30
H		360
G		300
F		720
B		540
Skip		~~60~~

2) Ball beads:

Kiwi lime Green		12 ball beads (12 mm) – for 12 holes at joint

Note: The colors presented above and on pictures are not precise to show the colors on the actual product.

2..........April Days

Element A: Letter Notation

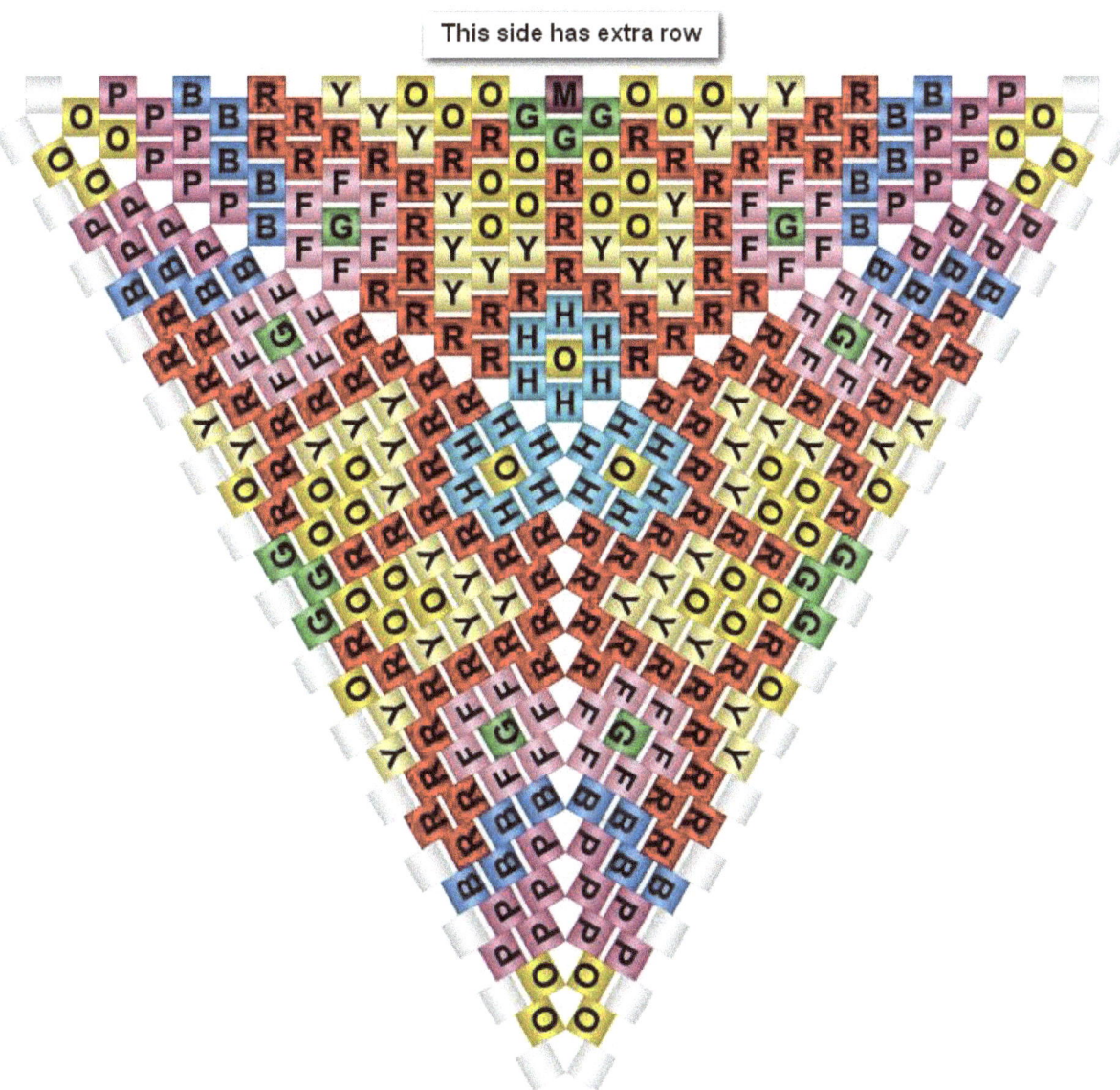

Important: All the white indicators on the graphic are location marking only. There are no beads needed for the places. Please skip all of them by following the element build instruction.

Element A: Instruction

Total 15 rows

Row 1 :   3H.

Row 2 :   2H, 2H, 2H.

Row 3 :   2R, 1O. 2R, 1O. 2R, 1O.

Row 4 :   2R, 1H, 1H. 2R, 1H, 1H. 2R, 1H, 1H.

Row 5 :   2R, 1R, 1H, 1R. 2R, 1R, 1H, 1R. 2R, 1R, 1H, 1R.

Row 6 :   2R, 1Y, 1R, 1R, 1Y. 2R, 1Y, 1R, 1R, 1Y. 2R, 1Y, 1R, 1R, 1Y.

Row 7 :   2F, 1R, 1Y, 1R, 1Y, 1R. 2F, 1R, 1Y, 1R, 1Y, 1R. 2F, 1R, 1Y, 1R, 1Y, 1R.

Row 8 :   2F, 1F, 1Y, 1Y, 1Y, 1Y, 1F. 2F, 1F, 1Y, 1Y, 1Y, 1Y, 1F. 2F, 1F, 1Y, 1Y, 1Y, 1Y, 1F.

Row 9 :   2B, 1G, 1R, 1O, 1R, 1O, 1R, 1G. 2B, 1G, 1R, 1O, 1R, 1O, 1R, 1G.
2B, 1G, 1R, 1O, 1R, 1O, 1R, 1G.

Row 10 :   2P, 1F, 1F, 1Y, 1O, 1O, 1Y, 1F, 1F. 2P, 1F, 1F, 1Y, 1O, 1O, 1Y, 1F, 1F.
2P, 1F, 1F, 1Y, 1O, 1O, 1Y, 1F, 1F.

Row 11 :   2P, 1B, 1F, 1R, 1O, 1R, 1O, 1R, 1F, 1B. 2P, 1B, 1F, 1R, 1O, 1R, 1O, 1R, 1F, 1B.
2P, 1B, 1F, 1R, 1O, 1R, 1O, 1R, 1F, 1B.

Row 12 :   2P, 1B, 1R, 1R, 1R, 1O, 1O, 1R, 1R, 1R, 1B. 2P, 1B, 1R, 1R, 1R, 1O, 1O, 1R, 1R, 1R, 1B.
2P, 1B, 1R, 1R, 1R, 1O, 1O, 1R, 1R, 1R, 1B.

Row 13 :   2O, 1P, 1R, 1R, 1Y, 1R, 1G, 1R, 1Y, 1R, 1R, 1P. 2O, 1P, 1R, 1R, 1Y, 1R, 1G, 1R, 1Y, 1R, 1R, 1P.
2O, 1P, 1R, 1R, 1Y, 1R, 1G, 1R, 1Y, 1R, 1R, 1P.

Row 14 :   2O, 1P, 1B, 1R, 1Y, 1O, 1G, 1G, 1O, 1Y, 1R, 1B, 1P.
2O, 1P, 1B, 1R, 1Y, 1O, 1G, 1G, 1O, 1Y, 1R, 1B, 1P.
2O, 1P, 1B, 1R, 1Y, 1O, 1G, 1G, 1O, 1Y, 1R, 1B, 1P.

The following is the extra row:

Row 15 :   Skip, 1P, 1B, 1R, 1Y, 1O, 1O, 1M, 1O, 1O, 1Y, 1R, 1B, 1P.

Element A: Number Notation

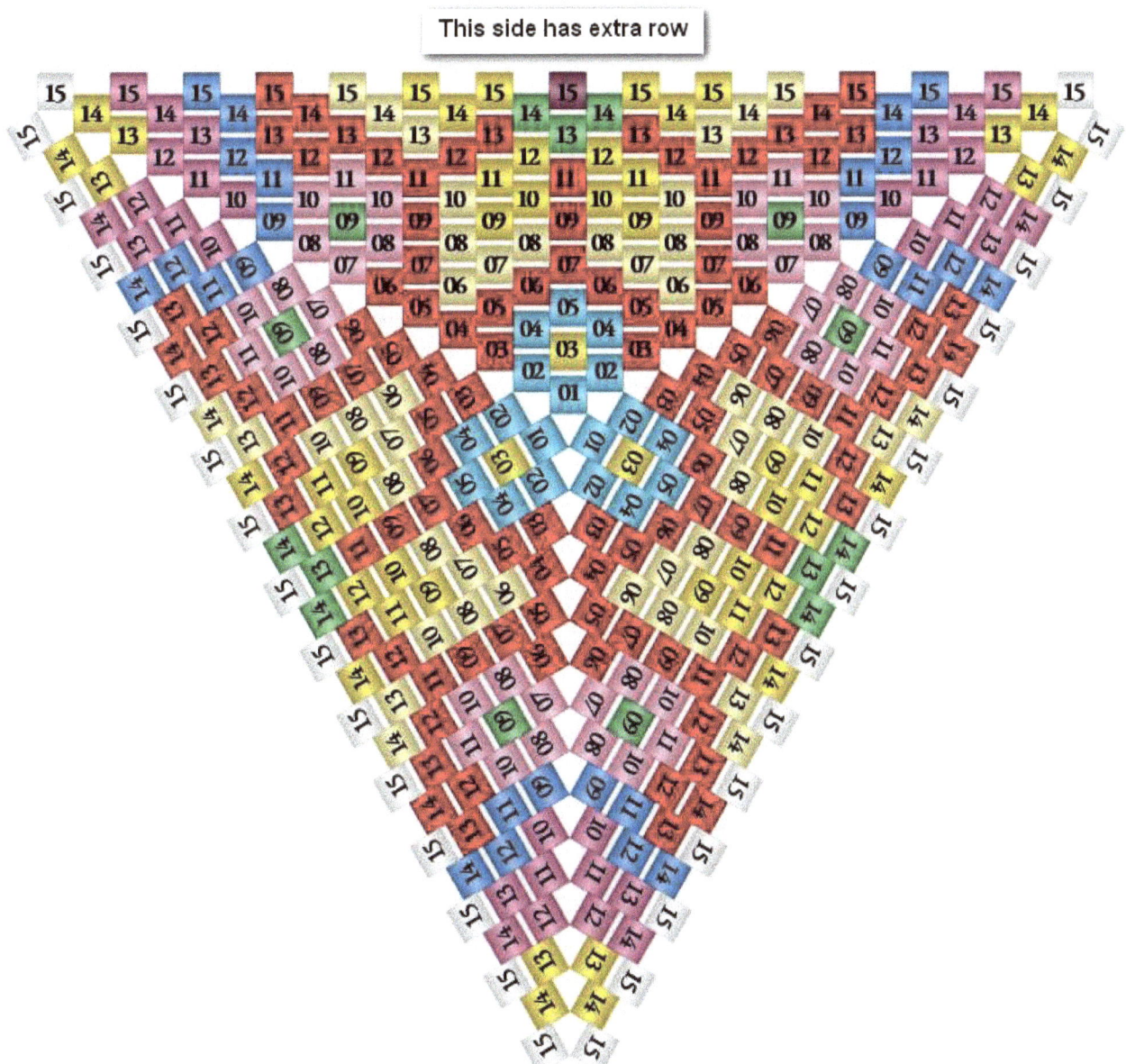

Important: All the white indicators on the graphic are location marking only. There are no beads needed for the places. Please skip all of them by following the element build instruction.

Element B: Letter Notation

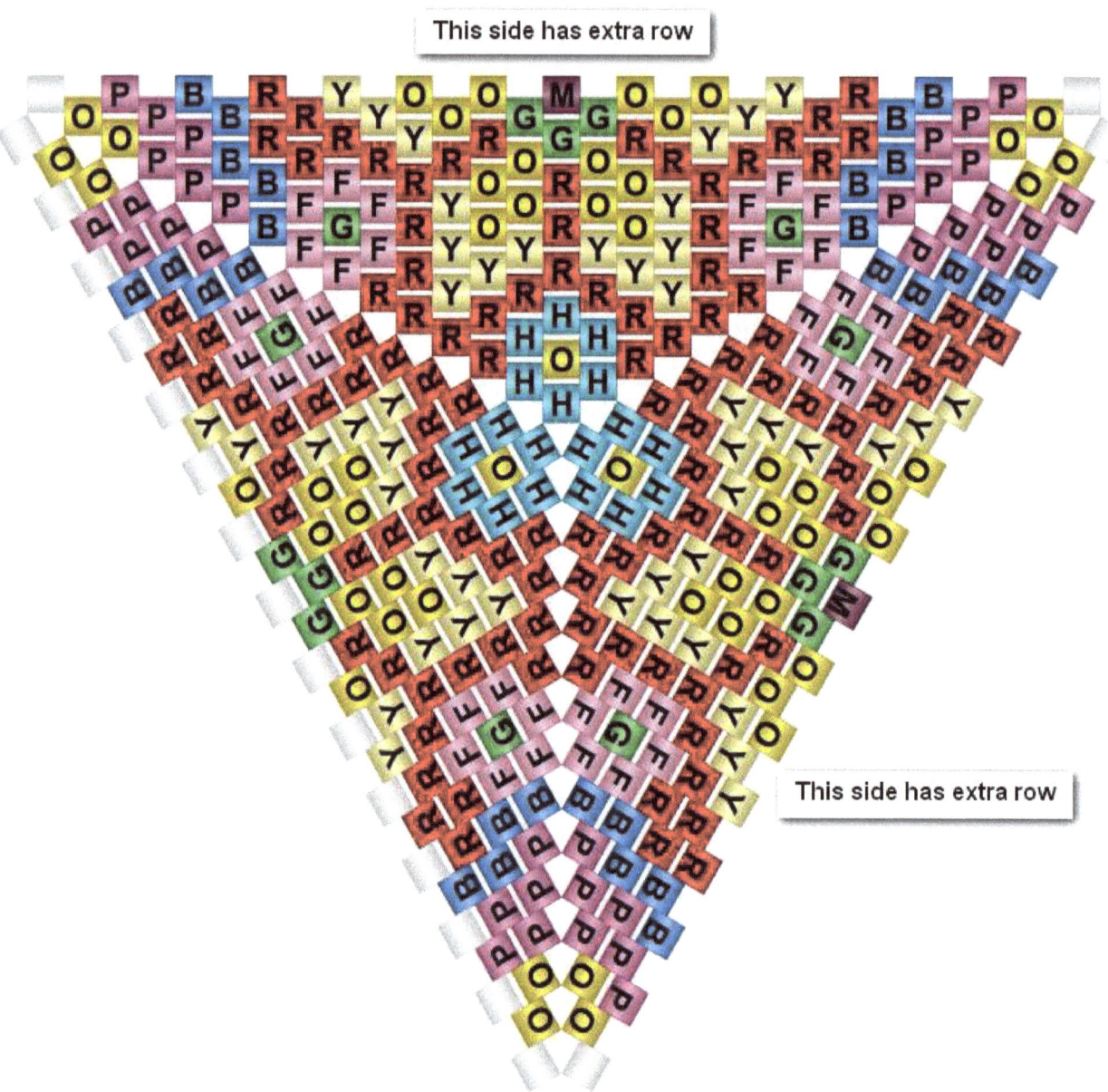

Important: All the white indicators on the graphic are location marking only. There are no beads needed for the places. Please skip all of them by following the element build instruction.

Element B: Instruction

Total 15 rows

Row 1 : 3H.

Row 2 : 2H, 2H, 2H.

Row 3 : 2R, 1O. 2R, 1O. 2R, 1O.

Row 4 : 2R, 1H, 1H. 2R, 1H, 1H. 2R, 1H, 1H.

Row 5 : 2R, 1R, 1H, 1R. 2R, 1R, 1H, 1R. 2R, 1R, 1H, 1R.

Row 6 : 2R, 1Y, 1R, 1R, 1Y. 2R, 1Y, 1R, 1R, 1Y. 2R, 1Y, 1R, 1R, 1Y.

Row 7 : 2F, 1R, 1Y, 1R, 1Y, 1R. 2F, 1R, 1Y, 1R, 1Y, 1R. 2F, 1R, 1Y, 1R, 1Y, 1R.

Row 8 : 2F, 1F, 1Y, 1Y, 1Y, 1Y, 1F. 2F, 1F, 1Y, 1Y, 1Y, 1Y, 1F. 2F, 1F, 1Y, 1Y, 1Y, 1Y, 1F.

Row 9 : 2B, 1G, 1R, 1O, 1R, 1O, 1R, 1G. 2B, 1G, 1R, 1O, 1R, 1O, 1R, 1G.
2B, 1G, 1R, 1O, 1R, 1O, 1R, 1G.

Row 10 : 2P, 1F, 1F, 1Y, 1O, 1O, 1Y, 1F, 1F. 2P, 1F, 1F, 1Y, 1O, 1O, 1Y, 1F, 1F.
2P, 1F, 1F, 1Y, 1O, 1O, 1Y, 1F, 1F.

Row 11 : 2P, 1B, 1F, 1R, 1O, 1R, 1O, 1R, 1F, 1B. 2P, 1B, 1F, 1R, 1O, 1R, 1O, 1R, 1F, 1B.
2P, 1B, 1F, 1R, 1O, 1R, 1O, 1R, 1F, 1B.

Row 12 : 2P, 1B, 1R, 1R, 1R, 1O, 1O, 1R, 1R, 1R, 1B. 2P, 1B, 1R, 1R, 1R, 1O, 1O, 1R, 1R, 1R, 1B.
2P, 1B, 1R, 1R, 1R, 1O, 1O, 1R, 1R, 1R, 1B.

Row 13 : 2O, 1P, 1R, 1R, 1Y, 1R, 1G, 1R, 1Y, 1R, 1R, 1P. 2O, 1P, 1R, 1R, 1Y, 1R, 1G, 1R, 1Y, 1R, 1R, 1P.
2O, 1P, 1R, 1R, 1Y, 1R, 1G, 1R, 1Y, 1R, 1R, 1P.

Row 14 : 2O, 1P, 1B, 1R, 1Y, 1O, 1G, 1G, 1O, 1Y, 1R, 1B, 1P.
2O, 1P, 1B, 1R, 1Y, 1O, 1G, 1G, 1O, 1Y, 1R, 1B, 1P.
2O, 1P, 1B, 1R, 1Y, 1O, 1G, 1G, 1O, 1Y, 1R, 1B, 1P.

The following is the extra row:

Row 15 Skip, 1P, 1B, 1R, 1Y, 1O, 1O, 1M, 1O, 1O, 1Y, 1R, 1B, 1P.
Skip, 1P, 1B, 1R, 1Y, 1O, 1O, 1M, 1O, 1O, 1Y, 1R, 1B, 1P.

Element B: Number Notation

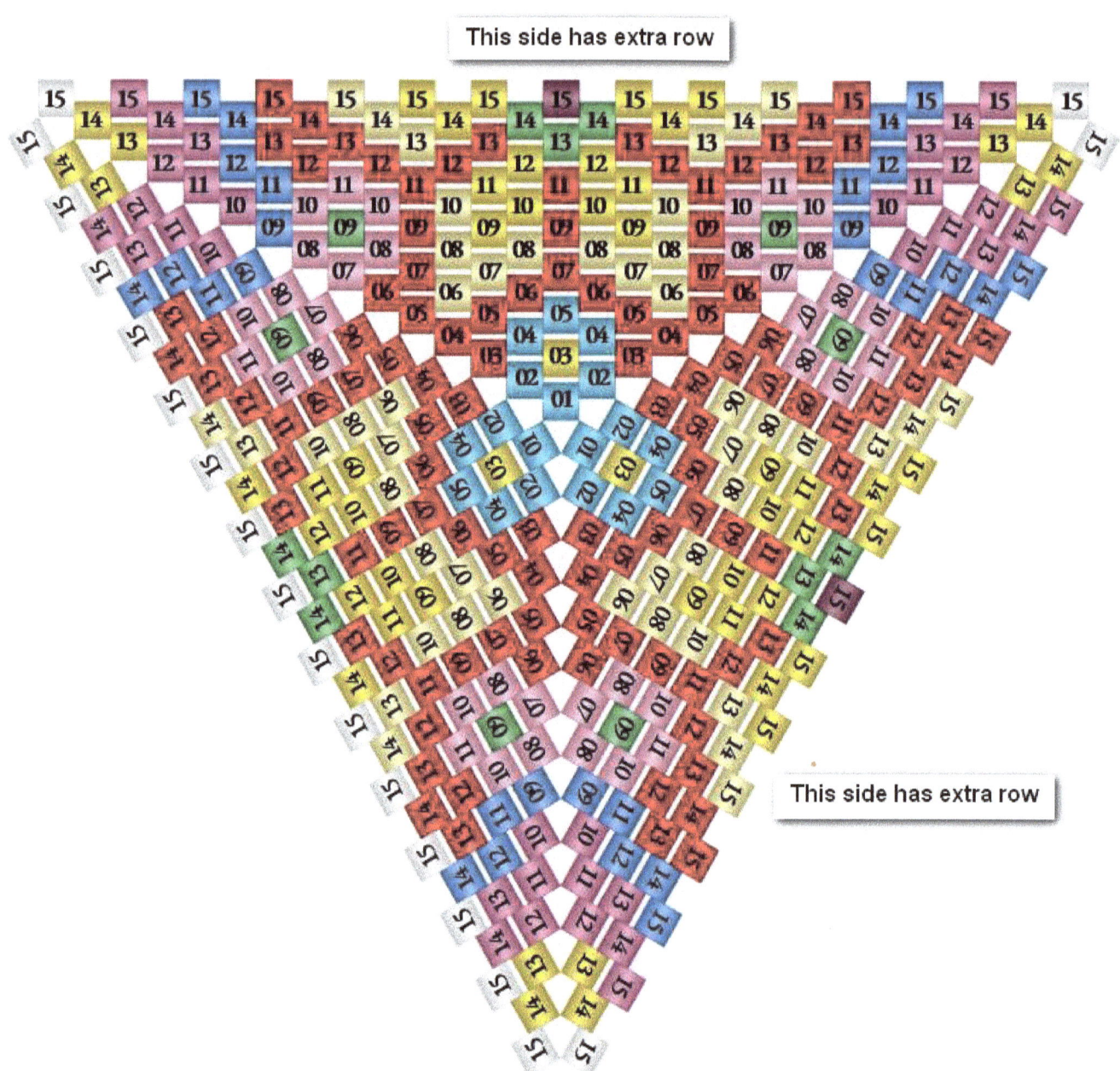

Important: All the white indicators on the graphic are location marking only. There are no beads needed for the places. Please skip all of them by following the element build instruction.

Join Two Triangle Pieces in Zigzag

Note: Please keep the extra string for sewing the ball bead later

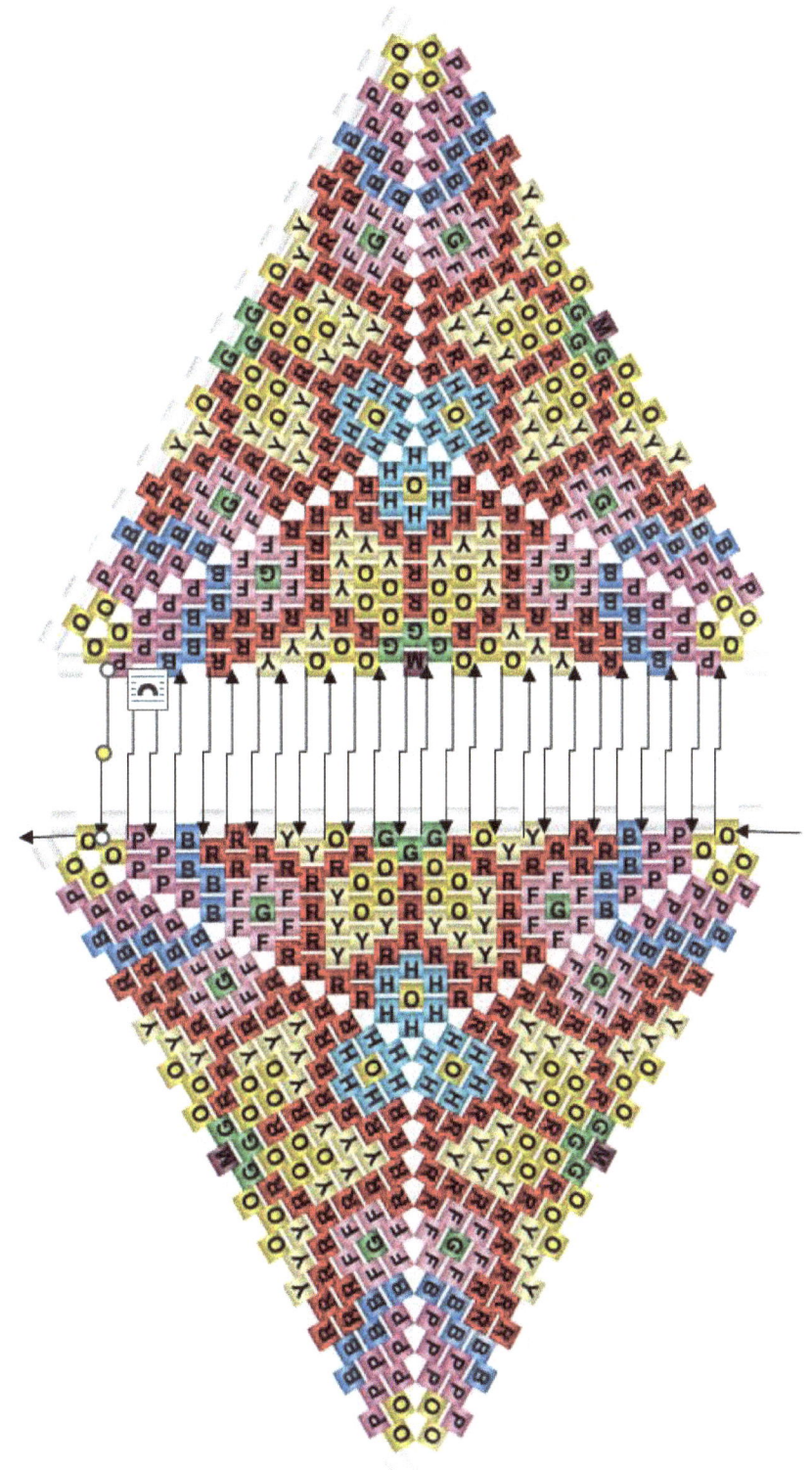

3D Beading Patterns..........9

3D Ball – All Piece Demo and Assembling Instruction

Element A:
- 10 pieces
- Please follow Element A instructions to bead. Note each piece has one side with extra row

Element B:
- 10 pieces
- Please follow Element B instructions to bead. Note each piece has two sides with extra row

Assembling:
- Please follow the pattern on the left to sew them together
- Before closing the last piece, fill in the ball with plank foam to keep the ball shape
- After all the 20 triangle pieces are assembled to a ball, sew the 12 mm ball beads to the holes at the joint pointers

Country Breeze

BALL DESCRIPTION:

15 rows, approximately the size of soccer ball, made with 20 pieces of triangles

MATERIALS

1. Perler Beads: 6,690 pieces, 9 colors
2. Ball Beads: 12 pieces, 12 mm in diameter, 1 color
3. Beading String: fishing line – 6 lbs. 145in for one triangle piece and the ball bead
4. Inside filling: used plank foam

TOOLS

1. Needle: size of 2.5 in
2. Curved needle: size of 3.5 in
3. Scissors
4. Stainless steel tweezer

Color and Number of Beads

1) Perler beads:

Symbol ID	Color preview	Count
Y		2 520
S		600
R		1 020
P		480
O		540
G		60
F		30
C		720
B		720
Skip		~~60~~

2) Ball beads:

Purple		12 ball beads (12 mm) – for 12 holes at joint

Note: The colors presented above and on pictures are not precise to show the colors on the actual product.

Element A: Letter Notation

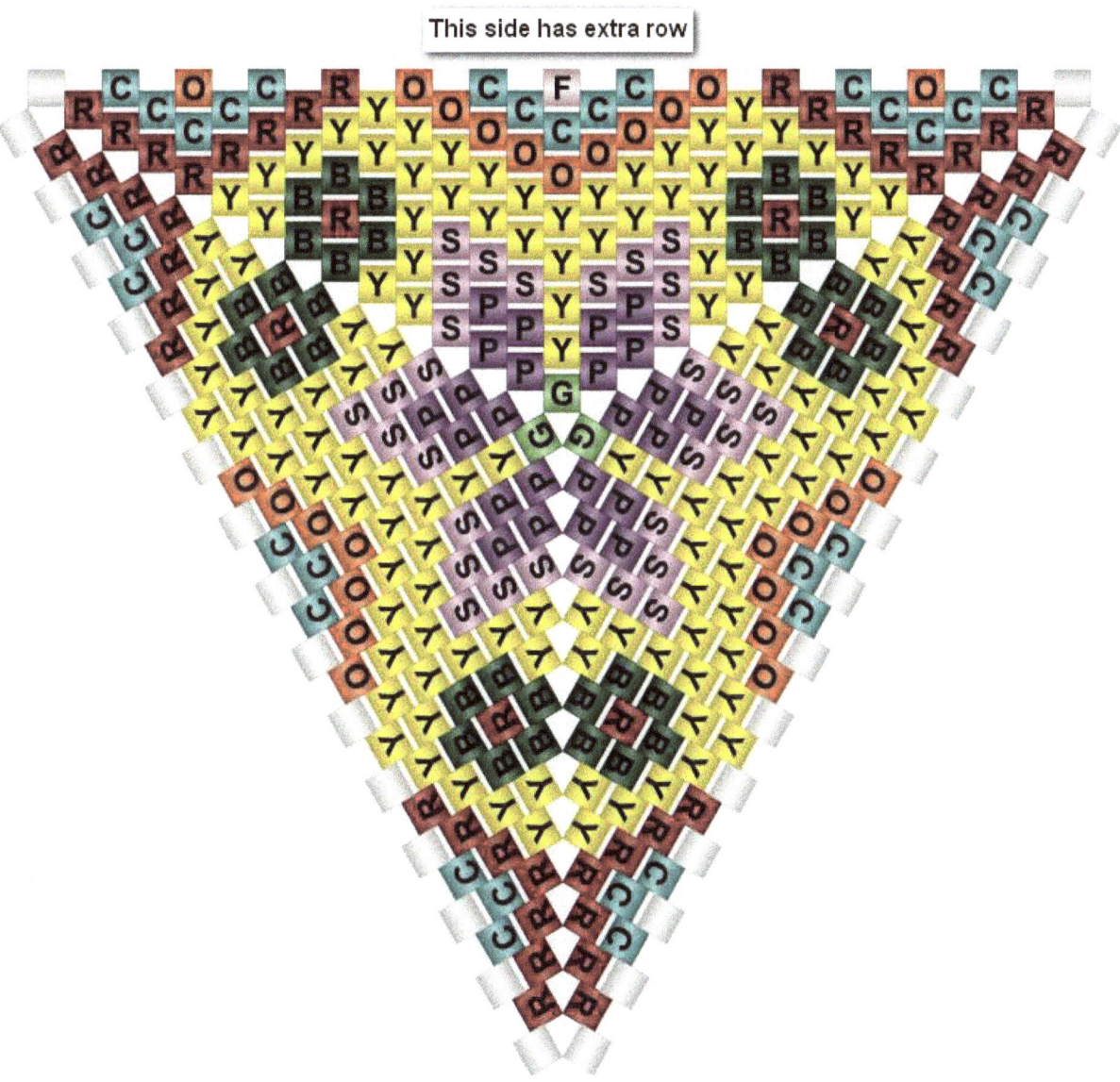

Important: All the white indicators on the graphic are location marking only. There are no beads needed for the places. Please skip all of them by following the element build instruction.

Element A: Instruction

Total 15 rows

Row 1: 3G

Row 2: 2P. 2P. 2P.

Row 3: 2P, 1Y. 2P, 1Y. 2P, 1Y.

Row 4: 2S, 1P, 1P. 2S, 1P, 1P. 2S, 1P, 1P.

Row 5: 2Y, 1P, 1Y, 1P. 2Y, 1P, 1Y, 1P. 2Y, 1P, 1Y, 1P.

Row 6: 2Y, 1S, 1S, 1S, 1S. 2Y, 1S, 1S, 1S, 1S. 2Y, 1S, 1S, 1S, 1S.

Row 7: 2B, 1Y, 1S, 1Y, 1S, 1Y. 2B, 1Y, 1S, 1Y, 1S, 1Y. 2B, 1Y, 1S, 1Y, 1S, 1Y.

Row 8: 2B, 1B, 1S, 1Y, 1Y, 1S, 1B. 2B, 1B, 1S, 1Y, 1Y, 1S, 1B. 2B, 1B, 1S, 1Y, 1Y, 1S, 1B.

Row 9: 2Y, 1R, 1Y, 1Y, 1Y, 1Y, 1Y, 1R. 2Y, 1R, 1Y, 1Y, 1Y, 1Y, 1Y, 1R. 2Y, 1R, 1Y, 1Y, 1Y, 1Y, 1Y, 1R.

Row 10: 2Y, 1B, 1B, 1Y, 1Y, 1Y, 1Y, 1B, 1B. 2Y, 1B, 1B, 1Y, 1Y, 1Y, 1Y, 1B, 1B.
 2Y, 1B, 1B, 1Y, 1Y, 1Y, 1Y, 1B, 1B.

Row 11: 2R, 1Y, 1B, 1Y, 1Y, 1O, 1Y, 1Y, 1B, 1Y. 2R, 1Y, 1B, 1Y, 1Y, 1O, 1Y, 1Y, 1B, 1Y.
2R, 1Y, 1B, 1Y, 1Y, 1O, 1Y, 1Y, 1B, 1Y.

Row 12: 2R, 1R, 1Y, 1Y, 1Y, 1O, 1O, 1Y, 1Y, 1Y, 1R. 2R, 1R, 1Y, 1Y, 1Y, 1O, 1O, 1Y, 1Y, 1Y, 1R.
2R, 1R, 1Y, 1Y, 1Y, 1O, 1O, 1Y, 1Y, 1Y, 1R.

Row 13: 2R ,1C, 1R, 1Y, 1Y, 1O, 1C, 1O, 1Y, 1Y, 1R, 1C. 2R ,1C, 1R, 1Y, 1Y, 1O, 1C, 1O, 1Y, 1Y, 1R, 1C.
2R ,1C, 1R, 1Y, 1Y, 1O, 1C, 1O, 1Y, 1Y, 1R, 1C.

Row 14: 2R, 1C, 1C, 1R, 1Y, 1O, 1C, 1C, 1O, 1Y, 1R, 1C, 1C.
2R, 1C, 1C, 1R, 1Y, 1O, 1C, 1C, 1O, 1Y, 1R, 1C, 1C.
2R, 1C, 1C, 1R, 1Y, 1O, 1C, 1C, 1O, 1Y, 1R, 1C, 1C.

The following is the extra row:

Row 15: SKIP, 1C, 1O, 1C, 1R, 1O, 1C, 1F, 1C, 1O, 1R, 1C, 1O, 1C.

Element A: Number Notation

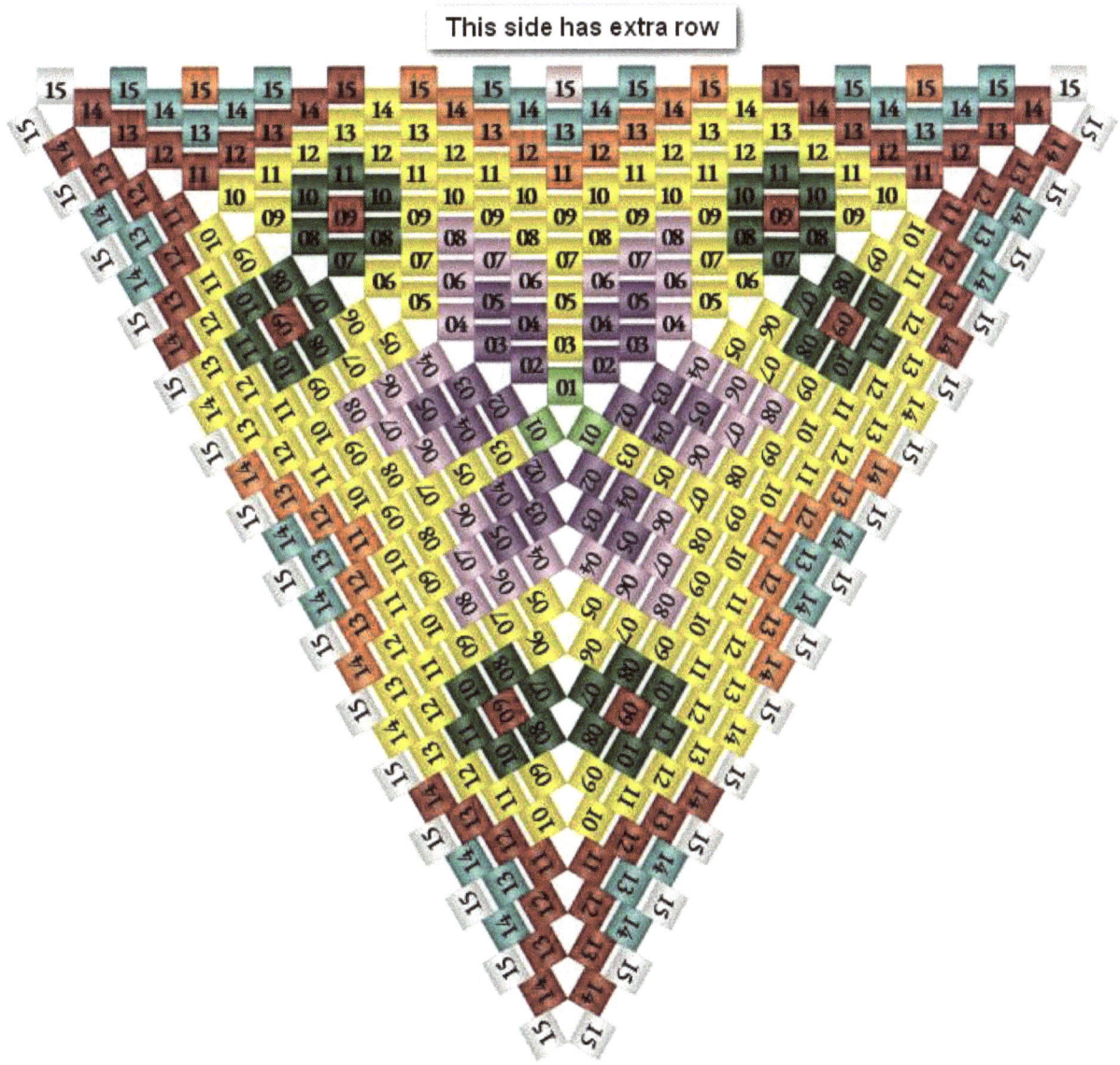

Important: All the white indicators on the graphic are location marking only. There are no beads needed for the places. Please skip all of them by following the element build instruction.

3D Beading Patterns..........15

Element B: Letter Notation

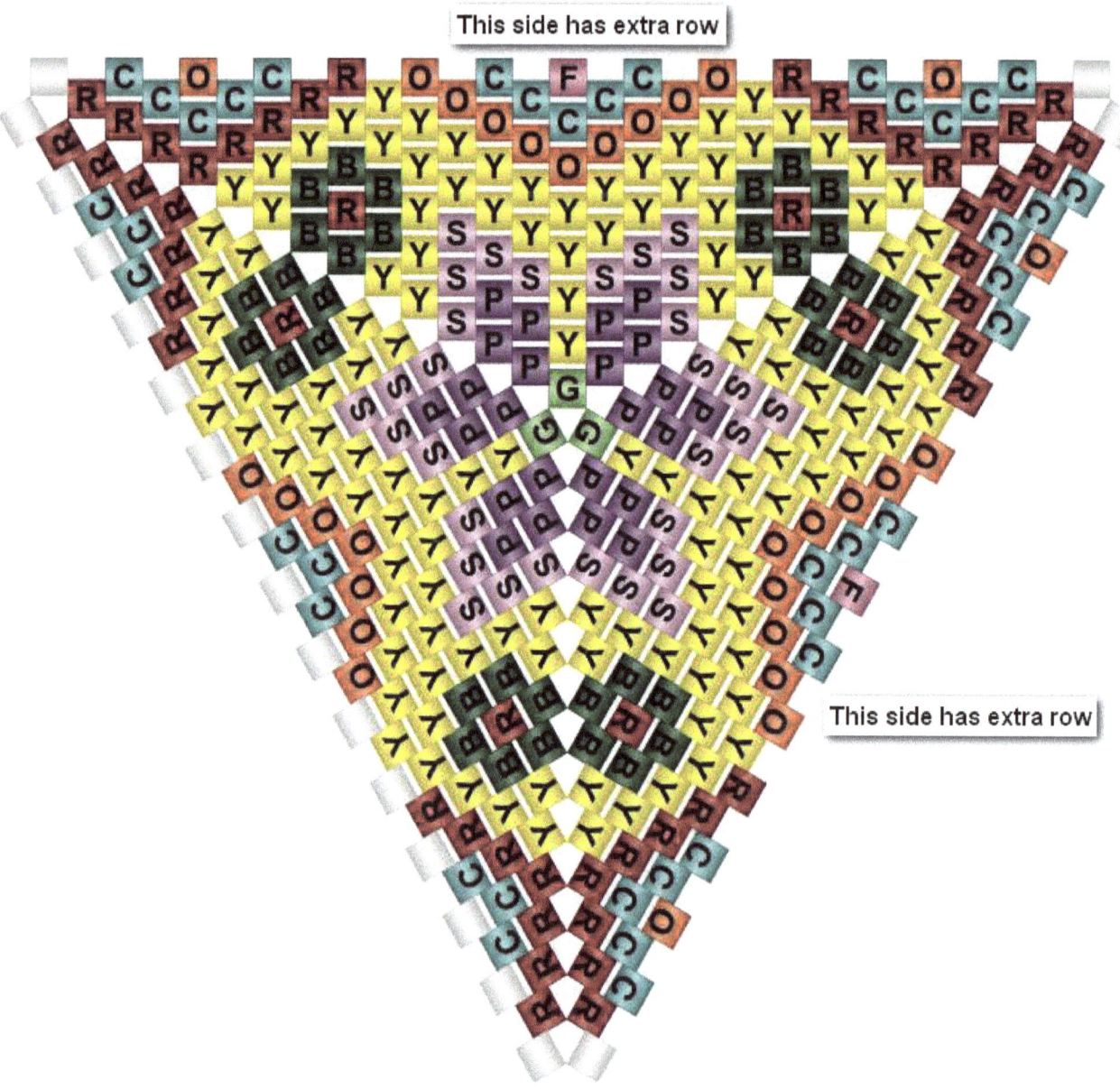

Important: All the white indicators on the graphic are location marking only. There are no beads needed for the places. Please skip all of them by following the element build instruction.

Element B: Instruction

Total 15 rows

Row 1: 3G

Row 2: 2P. 2P. 2P.

Row 3: 2P, 1Y. 2P, 1Y. 2P, 1Y.

Row 4: 2S, 1P, 1P. 2S, 1P, 1P. 2S, 1P, 1P.

Row 5: 2Y, 1P, 1Y, 1P. 2Y, 1P, 1Y, 1P. 2Y, 1P, 1Y, 1P.

Row 6: 2Y, 1S, 1S, 1S, 1S. 2Y, 1S, 1S, 1S, 1S. 2Y, 1S, 1S, 1S, 1S.

Eaw 7: 2B, 1Y, 1S, 1Y, 1S, 1Y. 2B, 1Y, 1S, 1Y, 1S, 1Y. 2B, 1Y, 1S, 1Y, 1S, 1Y.

Row 8: 2B, 1B, 1S, 1Y, 1Y, 1S, 1B. 2B, 1B, 1S, 1Y, 1Y, 1S, 1B. 2B, 1B, 1S, 1Y, 1Y, 1S, 1B.

Row 9: 2Y, 1R, 1Y, 1Y, 1Y, 1Y, 1Y, 1R. 2Y, 1R, 1Y, 1Y, 1Y, 1Y, 1Y, 1R.
2Y, 1R, 1Y, 1Y, 1Y, 1Y, 1Y, 1R.

Row 10: 2Y, 1B, 1B, 1Y, 1Y, 1Y, 1Y, 1B, 1B. 2Y, 1B, 1B, 1Y, 1Y, 1Y, 1Y, 1B, 1B.
2Y, 1B, 1B, 1Y, 1Y, 1Y, 1Y, 1B, 1B.

Row 11: 2R, 1Y, 1B, 1Y, 1Y, 1O, 1Y, 1Y, 1B, 1Y. 2R, 1Y, 1B, 1Y, 1Y, 1O, 1Y, 1Y, 1B, 1Y.
2R, 1Y, 1B, 1Y, 1Y, 1O, 1Y, 1Y, 1B, 1Y.

Row 12: 2R, 1R, 1Y, 1Y, 1Y, 1O, 1O, 1Y, 1Y, 1Y, 1R. 2R, 1R, 1Y, 1Y, 1Y, 1O, 1O, 1Y, 1Y, 1Y, 1R.
2R, 1R, 1Y, 1Y, 1Y, 1O, 1O, 1Y, 1Y, 1Y, 1R.

Row 13: 2R ,1C, 1R, 1Y, 1Y, 1O, 1C, 1O, 1Y, 1Y, 1R, 1C.
2R ,1C, 1R, 1Y, 1Y, 1O, 1C, 1O, 1Y, 1Y, 1R, 1C.
2R ,1C, 1R, 1Y, 1Y, 1O, 1C, 1O, 1Y, 1Y, 1R, 1C.

Row 14: 2R, 1C, 1C, 1R, 1Y, 1O, 1C, 1C, 1O, 1Y, 1R, 1C, 1C.
2R, 1C, 1C, 1R, 1Y, 1O, 1C, 1C, 1O, 1Y, 1R, 1C, 1C.
2R, 1C, 1C, 1R, 1Y, 1O, 1C, 1C, 1O, 1Y, 1R, 1C, 1C.

The following is the extra row:

Row 15: SKIP, 1C, 1O, 1C, 1R, 1O, 1C, F, 1C, 1O, 1R, 1C, 1O, 1C.
SKIP, 1C, 1O, 1C, 1R, 1O, 1C, 1F, 1C, 1O, 1R, 1C, 1O, 1C.

Element B: Number Notation

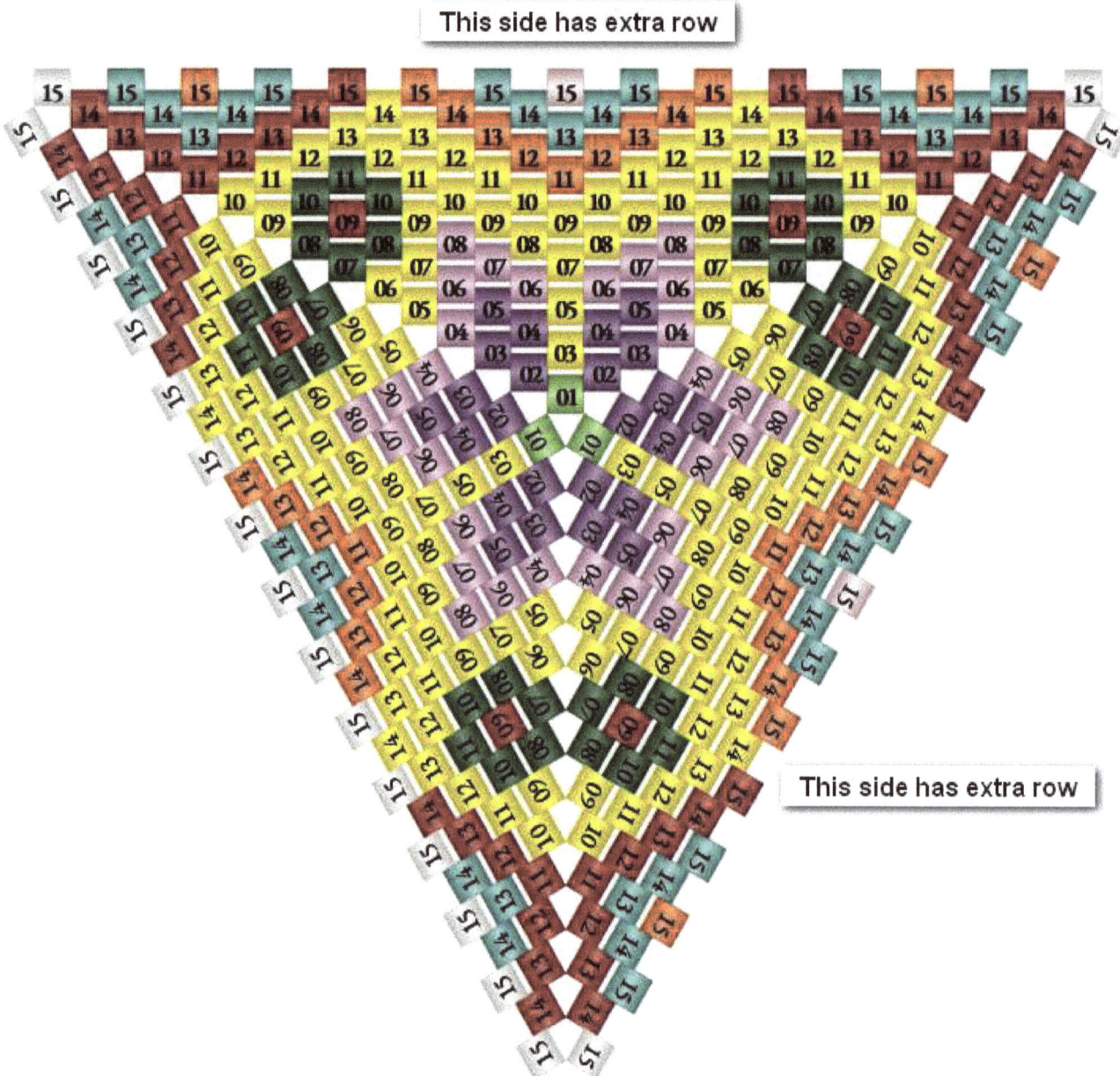

Important: All the white indicators on the graphic are location marking only. There are no beads needed for the places. Please skip all of them by following the element build instruction.

Join Two Triangle Pieces in Zigzag

Note: Please keep the extra string for sewing the ball bead later

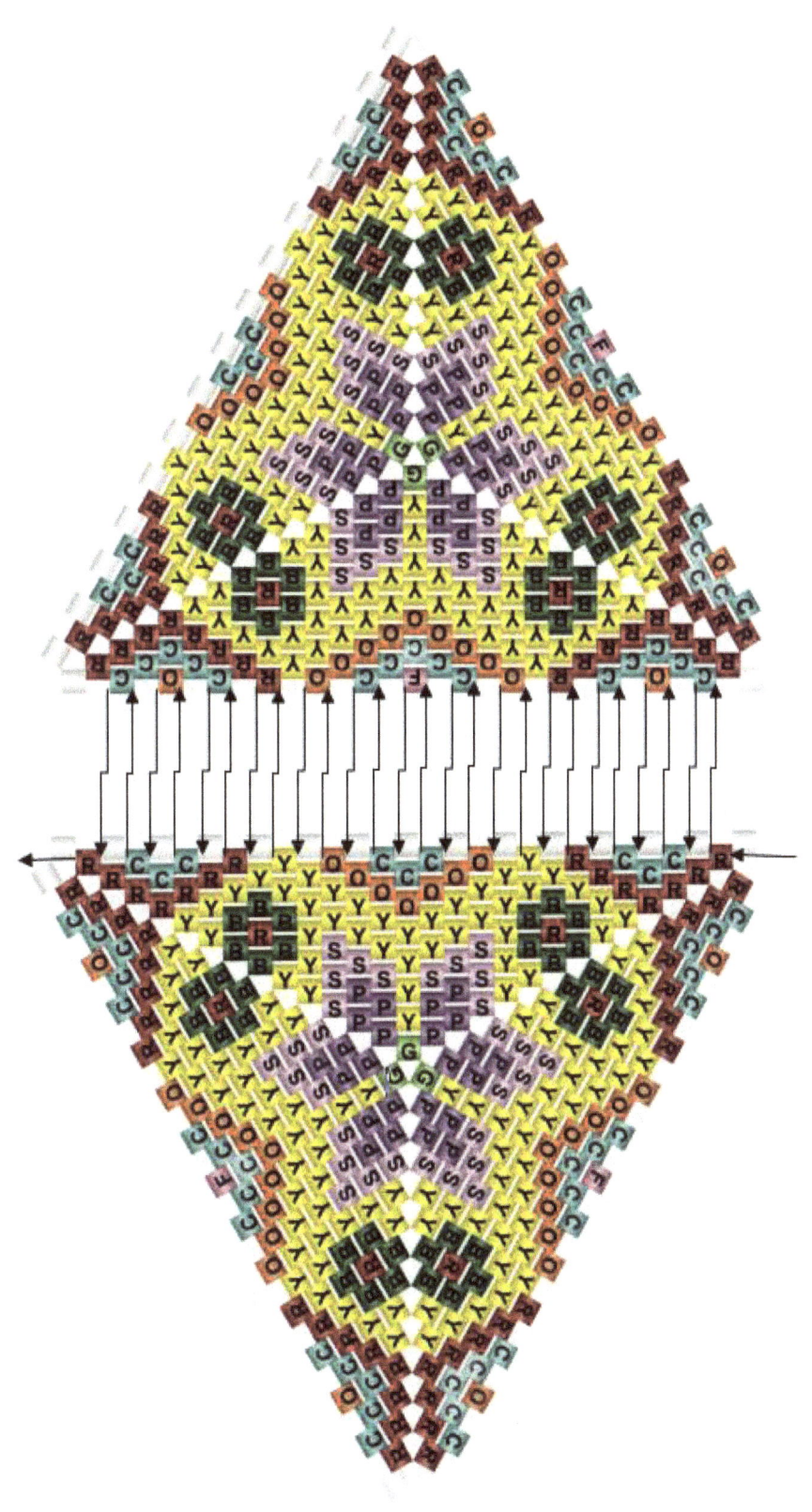

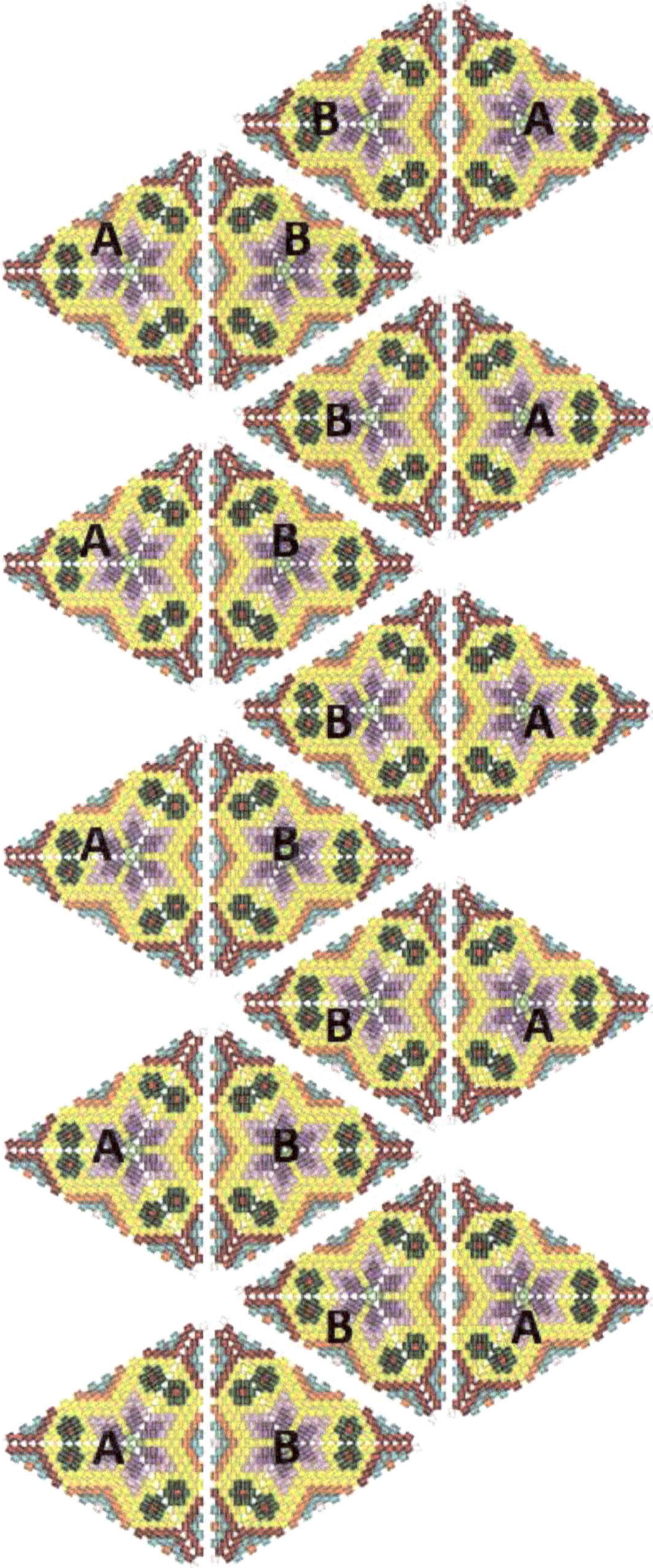

3D Ball – All Piece Demo and Assembling Instruction

Element A:
- 10 pieces
- Please follow Element A instructions to bead. Note each piece has one side with extra row

Element B:
- 10 pieces
- Please follow Element B instructions to bead. Note each piece has two sides with extra row

Assembling:
- Please follow the pattern on the left to sew them together
- Before closing the last piece, fill in the ball with plank foam to keep the ball shape
- After all the 20 triangle pieces are assembled to a ball, sew the 12 mm ball beads to the holes at the joint pointers

Night Lure

BALL DESCRIPTION:

15 rows, approximately the size of soccer ball, made with 20 pieces of triangles

MATERIALS

1. Perler Beads: 6,690 pieces, 8 colors
2. Ball Beads: 12 pieces, 12 mm in diameter, 1 color
3. Beading String: fishing line – 6 lbs. 145in for one triangle piece and the ball bead
4. Inside filling: used plank foam

TOOLS

1. Needle: size of 2.5 in
2. Curved needle: size of 3.5 in
3. Scissors
4. Stainless steel tweezer

Color and Number of Beads

1) Perler beads:

Symbol ID	Color preview	Count
C		360
B		3 120
P		900
O		780
R		720
E		360
G		240
Y		210
Skip		~~60~~

2) Ball beads:

Kiwi lime Green		12 ball beads (12 mm) – for 12 holes at joint

Note: The colors presented above and on pictures are not precise to show the colors on the actual product.

Element A: Letter Notation

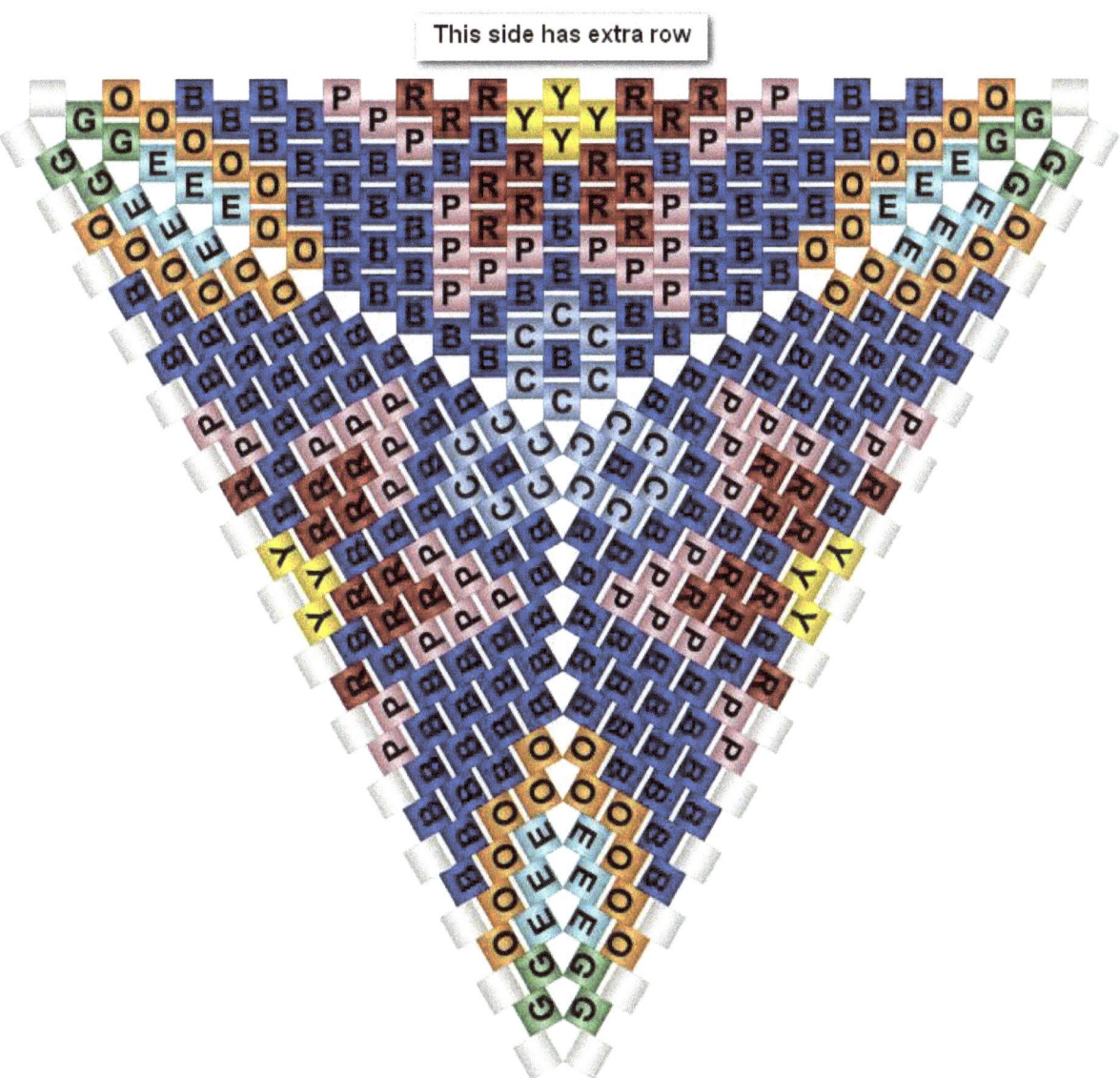

Important: All the white indicators on the graphic are location marking only. There are no beads needed for the places. Please skip all of them by following the element build instruction.

3D Beading Patterns..........23

Element A: Instruction

Total 15 rows

Row 1:   3C.

Row 2:   2C. 2C. 2C.

Row 3:   2B, 1B. 2B, 1B. 2B, 1B.

Row 4:   2B, 1C, 1C. 2B, 1C, 1C. 2B, 1C, 1C.

Row 5:   2B, 1B, 1C, 1B. 2B, 1B, 1C, 1B. 2B, 1B, 1C, 1B.

Row 6:   2B, 1P, 1B, 1B, 1P. 2B, 1P, 1B, 1B, 1P. 2B, 1P, 1B, 1B, 1P.

Row 7:   2B, 1B, 1P, 1B, 1P, 1B. 2B, 1B, 1P, 1B, 1P, 1B.   2B, 1B, 1P, 1B, 1P, 1B.

Row 8:   2O, 1B, 1P, 1P, 1P, 1P, 1B. 2O, 1B, 1P, 1P, 1P, 1P, 1B. 2O, 1B, 1P, 1P, 1P, 1P, 1B.

Row 9:   2O, 1B, 1B, 1R, 1B, 1R, 1B, 1B. 2O, 1B, 1B, 1R, 1B, 1R, 1B, 1B. 2O, 1B, 1B, 1R, 1B, 1R, 1B, 1B.

Row 10:   2E, 1B, 1B, 1P, 1R, 1R, 1P, 1B, 1B. 2E, 1B, 1B, 1P, 1R, 1R, 1P, 1B, 1B.
2E, 1B, 1B, 1P, 1R, 1R, 1P, 1B, 1B.

Row 11:   2E, 1O, 1B, 1B, 1R, 1B, 1R, 1B, 1B, 1O. 2E, 1O, 1B, 1B, 1R, 1B, 1R, 1B, 1B, 1O.
2E, 1O, 1B, 1B, 1R, 1B, 1R, 1B, 1B, 1O.

Row 12:   2E, 1O, 1B, 1B, 1B, 1R, 1R, 1B, 1B, 1B, 1O. 2E, 1O, 1B, 1B, 1B, 1R, 1R, 1B, 1B, 1B, 1O.
2E, 1O, 1B, 1B, 1B, 1R, 1R, 1B, 1B, 1B, 1O.

Row 13:   2G, 1O, 1B, 1B, 1P, B, 1Y, 1B, 1P, 1B, 1B, 1O. 2G, 1O, 1B, 1B, 1P, B, 1Y, 1B, 1P, 1B, 1B, 1O.
2G, 1O, 1B, 1B, 1P, B, 1Y, 1B, 1P, 1B, 1B, 1O.

Row 14:   2G, 1O, 1B, 1B, 1P, 1R, 1Y, 1Y, 1R, 1P, 1B, 1B, 1O.
2G, 1O, 1B, 1B, 1P, 1R, 1Y, 1Y, 1R, 1P, 1B, 1B, 1O.
2G, 1O, 1B, 1B, 1P, 1R, 1Y, 1Y, 1R, 1P, 1B, 1B, 1O.

The following is the extra row:

Row 15:   Skip, 1O, 1B, 1B, 1P, 1R, 1R, 1Y, 1R, 1R, 1P, 1B, 1B, 1O.

Element A: Number Notation

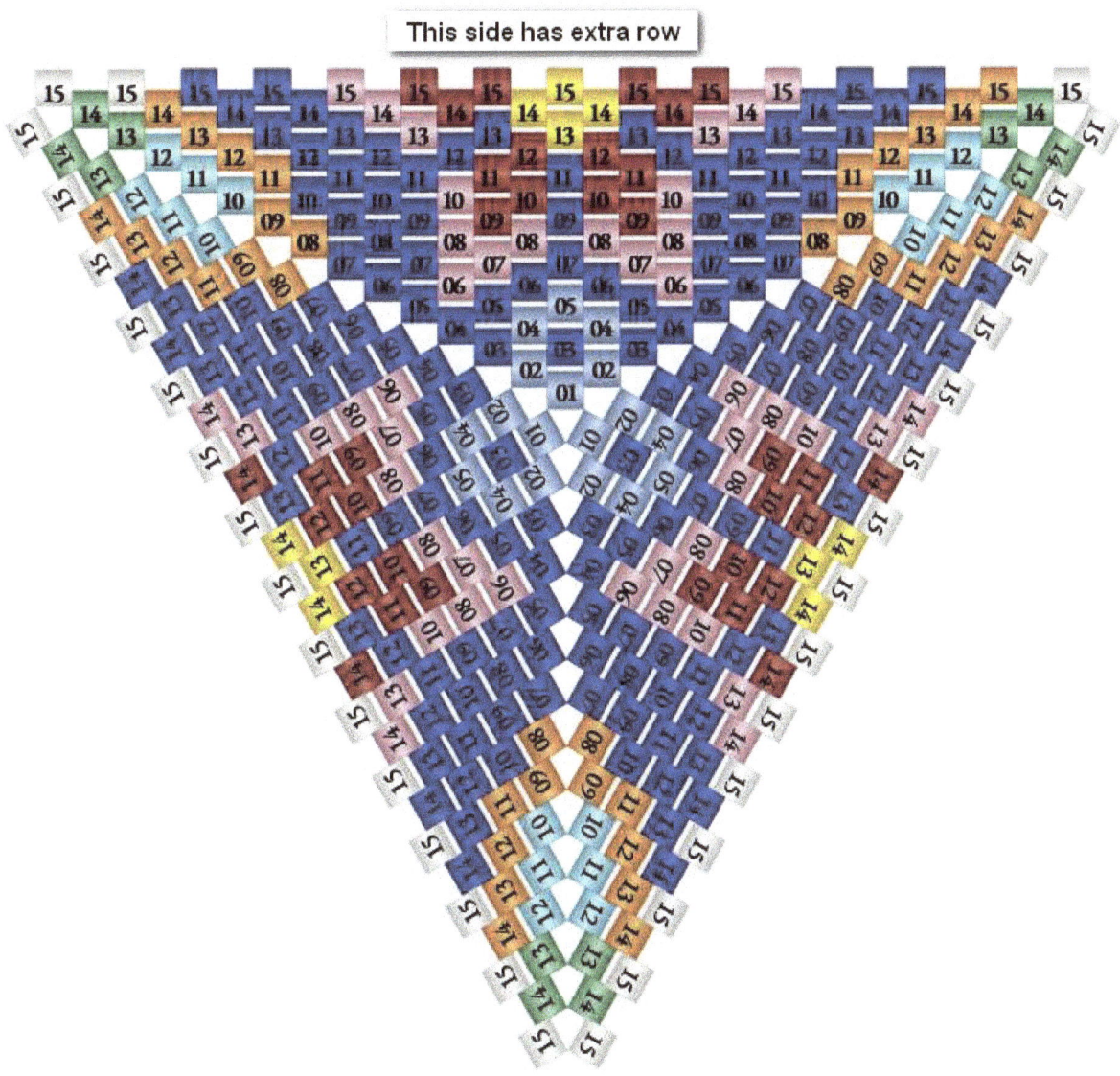

Important: All the white indicators on the graphic are location marking only. There are no beads needed for the places. Please skip all of them by following the element build instruction.

Element B: Letter Notation

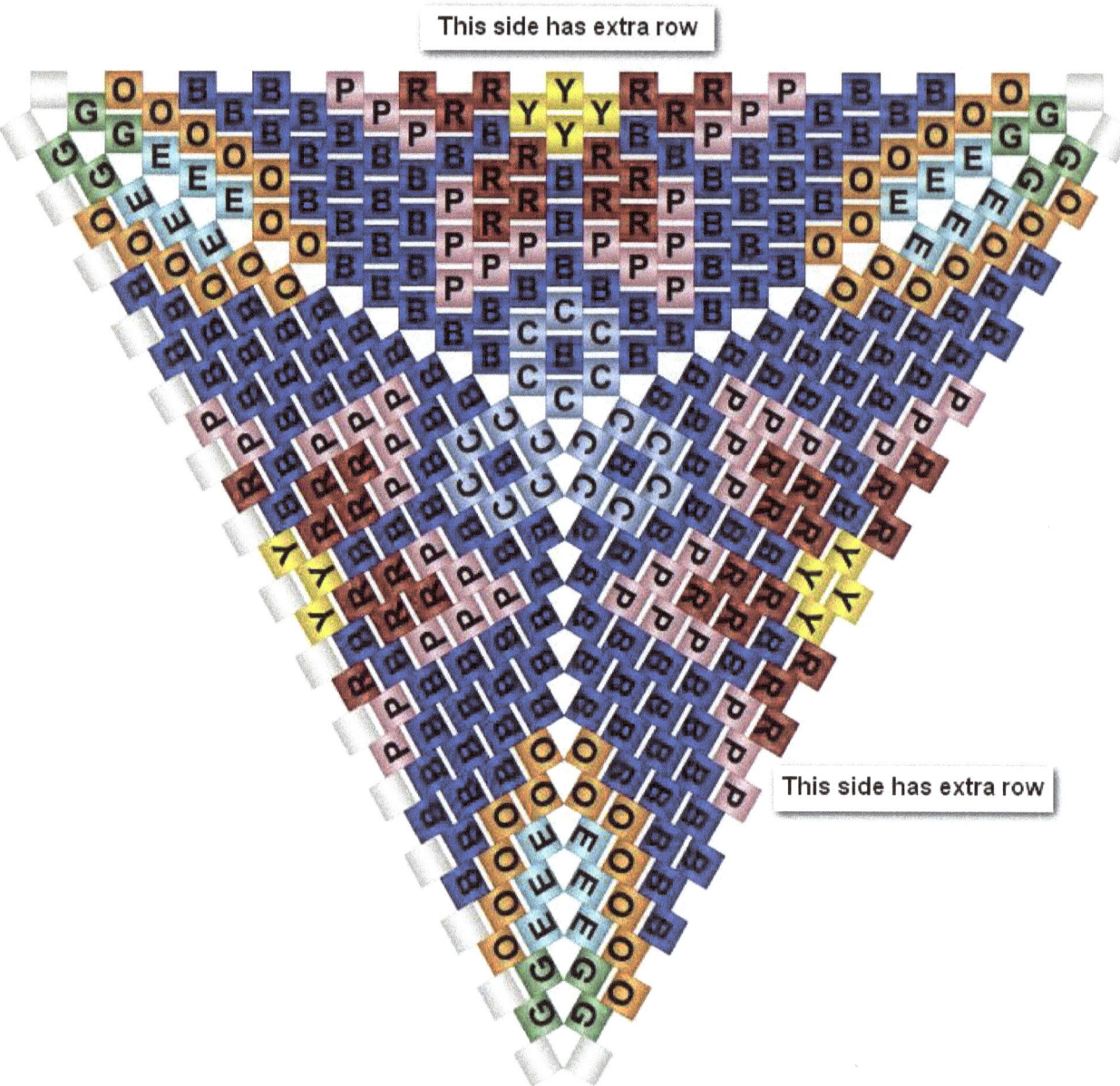

Important: All the white indicators on the graphic are location marking only. There are no beads needed for the places. Please skip all of them by following the element build instruction.

26..........April Days

Element B: Instruction

Total 15 rows

Row 1: 3C.

Row 2: 2C. 2C. 2C.

Row 3: 2B, 1B. 2B, 1B. 2B, 1B.

Row 4: 2B, 1C, 1C. 2B, 1C, 1C. 2B, 1C, 1C.

Row 5: 2B, 1B, 1C, 1B. 2B, 1B, 1C, 1B. 2B, 1B, 1C, 1B.

Row 6: 2B, 1P, 1B, 1B, 1P. 2B, 1P, 1B, 1B, 1P. 2B, 1P, 1B, 1B, 1P.

Row 7: 2B, 1B, 1P, 1B, 1P, 1B. 2B, 1B, 1P, 1B, 1P, 1B. 2B, 1B, 1P, 1B, 1P, 1B.

Row 8: 2O, 1B, 1P, 1P, 1P, 1P, 1B. 2O, 1B, 1P, 1P, 1P, 1P, 1B. 2O, 1B, 1P, 1P, 1P, 1P, 1B.

Row 9: 2O, 1B, 1B, 1R, 1B, 1R, 1B, 1B. 2O, 1B, 1B, 1R, 1B, 1R, 1B, 1B. 2O, 1B, 1B, 1R, 1B, 1R, 1B, 1B.

Row 10: 2E, 1B, 1B, 1P, 1R, 1R, 1P, 1B, 1B. 2E, 1B, 1B, 1P, 1R, 1R, 1P, 1B, 1B.
2E, 1B, 1B, 1P, 1R, 1R, 1P, 1B, 1B.

Row 11: 2E, 1O, 1B, 1B, 1R, 1B, 1R, 1B, 1B, 1O. 2E, 1O, 1B, 1B, 1R, 1B, 1R, 1B, 1B, 1O.
2E, 1O, 1B, 1B, 1R, 1B, 1R, 1B, 1B, 1O.

Row 12: 2E, 1O, 1B, 1B, 1B, 1R, 1R, 1B, 1B, 1O. 2E, 1O, 1B, 1B, 1B, 1R, 1R, 1B, 1B, 1B, 1O.
2E, 1O, 1B, 1B, 1B, 1R, 1R, 1B, 1B, 1O.

Row 13: 2G, 1O, 1B, 1B, 1P, B, 1Y, 1B, 1P, 1B, 1B, 1O. 2G, 1O, 1B, 1B, 1P, B, 1Y, 1B, 1P, 1B, 1B, 1O.
2G, 1O, 1B, 1B, 1P, B, 1Y, 1B, 1P, 1B, 1B, 1O.

Row 14: 2G, 1O, 1B, 1B, 1P, 1R, 1Y, 1Y, 1R, 1P, 1B, 1B, 1O.
2G, 1O, 1B, 1B, 1P, 1R, 1Y, 1Y, 1R, 1P, 1B, 1B, 1O.
2G, 1O, 1B, 1B, 1P, 1R, 1Y, 1Y, 1R, 1P, 1B, 1B, 1O.

The following is the extra row:

Row 15: Skip, 1O, 1B, 1B, 1P, 1R, 1R, 1Y, 1R, 1R, 1P, 1B, 1B, 1O.
Skip, 1O, 1B, 1B, 1P, 1R, 1R, 1Y, 1R, 1R, 1P, 1B, 1B, 1O.

Element B: Number Notation

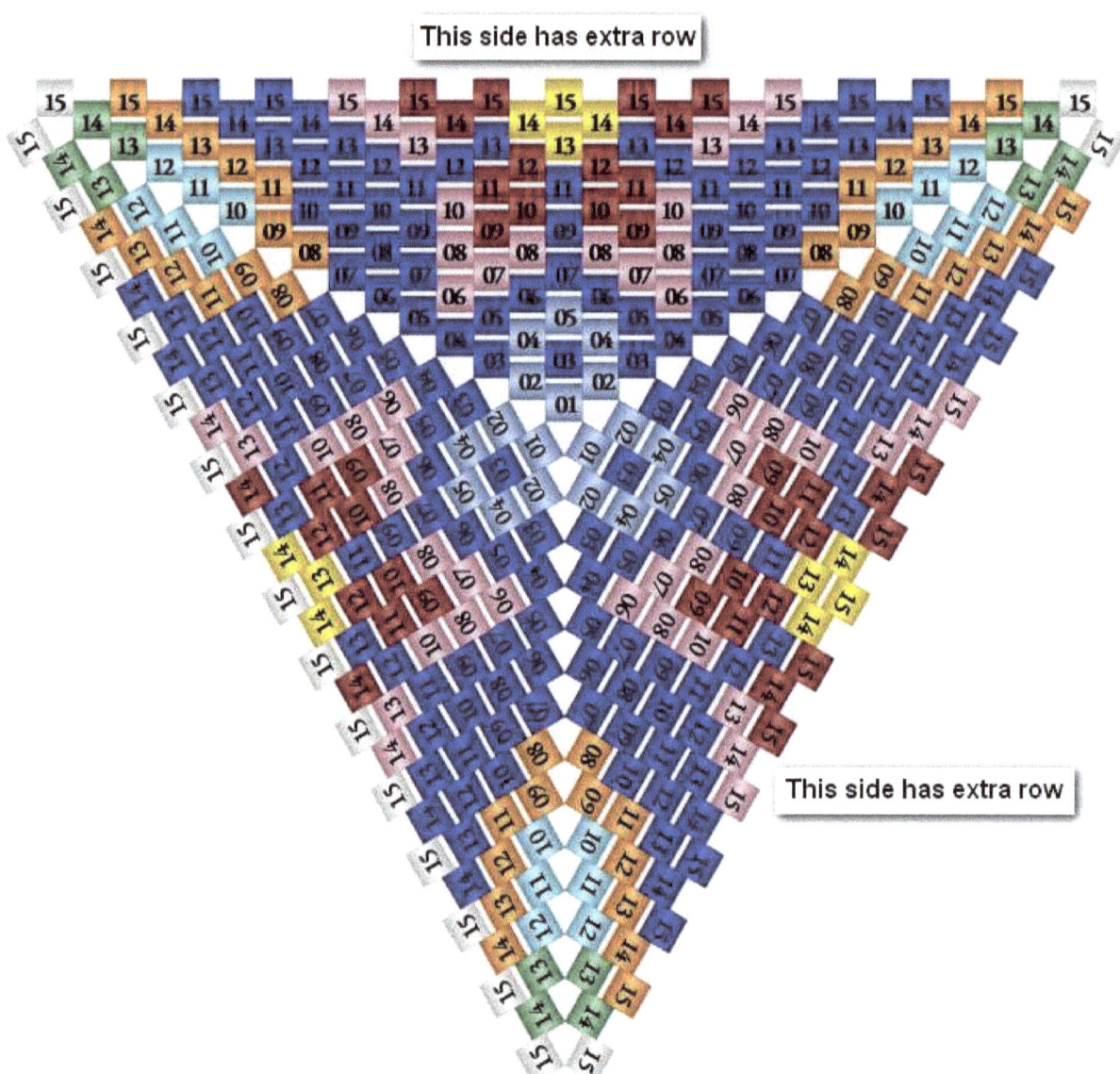

Important: All the white indicators on the graphic are location marking only. There are no beads needed for the places. Please skip all of them by following the element build instruction.

28..........April Days

Join Two Triangle Pieces in Zigzag

Note: Please keep the extra string for sewing the ball bead later

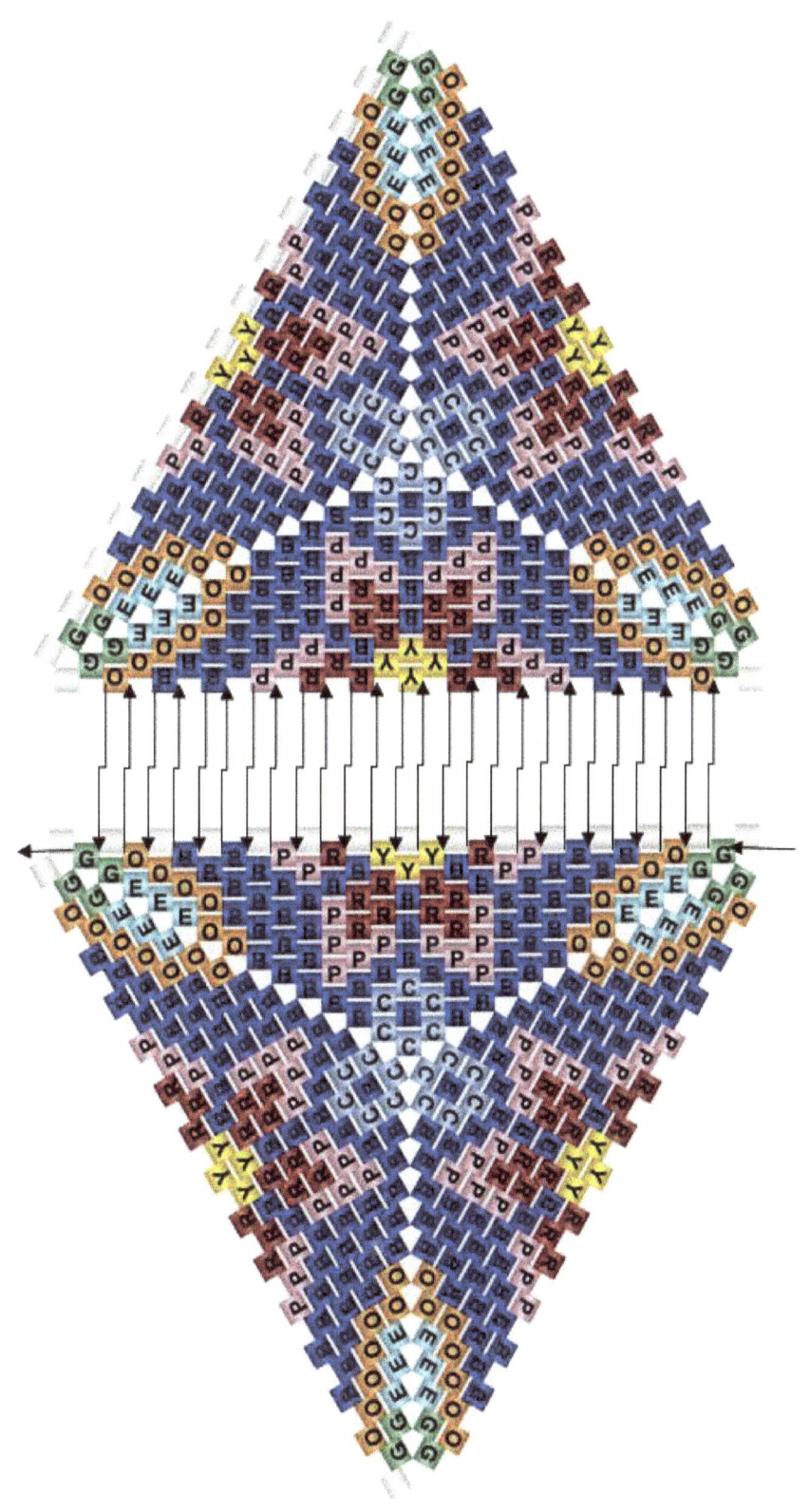

3D Beading Patterns..........29

3D Ball – All Piece Demo and Assembling Instruction

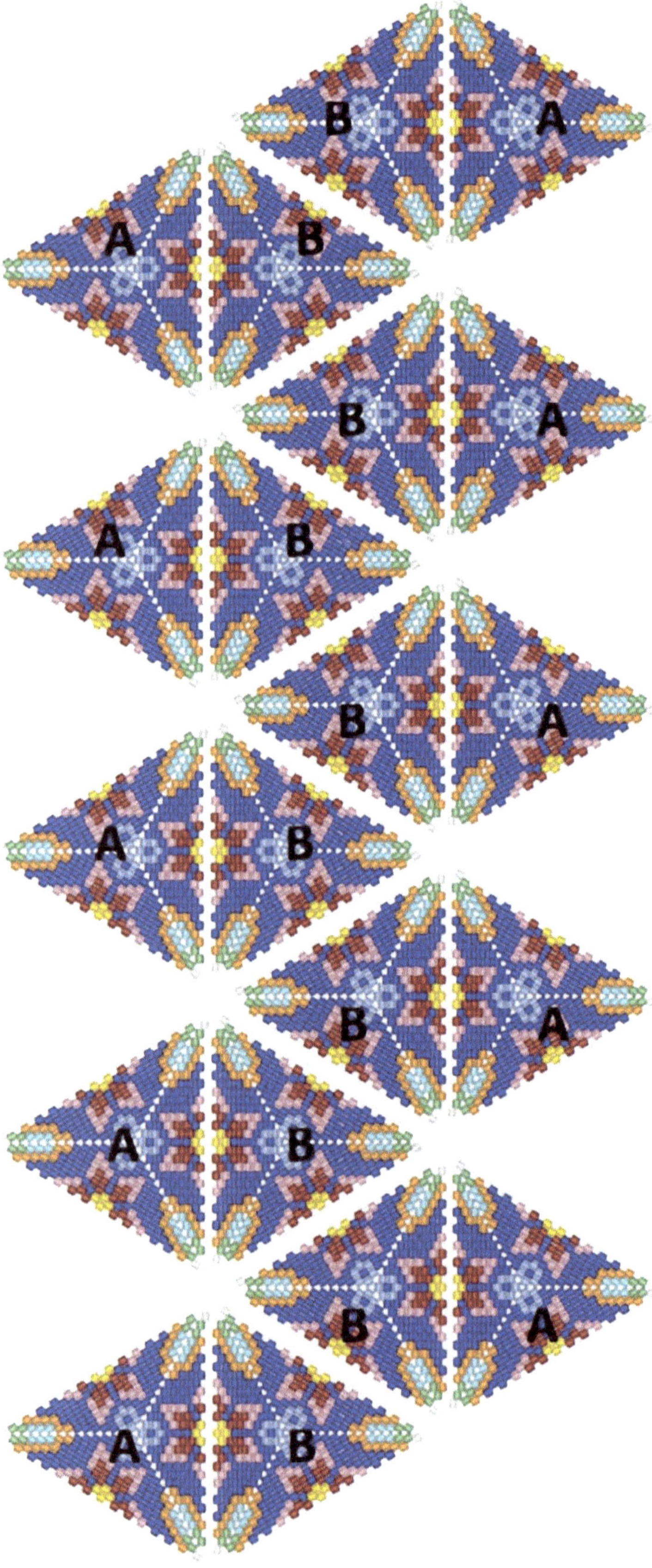

Element A:
- 10 pieces
- Please follow Element A instructions to bead. Note each piece has one side with extra row

Element B:
- 10 pieces
- Please follow Element B instructions to bead. Note each piece has two sides with extra row

Assembling:
- Please follow the pattern on the left to sew them together
- Before closing the last piece, fill in the ball with plank foam to keep the ball shape
- Sew the 12 mm ball beads to the holes at the joint pointers

30..........April Days

Desert Green

BALL DESCRIPTION:

16 rows, approximately the size of soccer ball, made with 20 pieces of triangles

MATERIALS

1. Perler Beads: 7,620 pieces, 11 colors
2. Ball Beads: 12 pieces, 12 mm in diameter, 1 color
3. Beading String: fishing line – 6 lbs. 160 in for one triangle piece and the ball bead
4. Inside filling: used plank foam

TOOLS

1. Needle: size of 2.5 in
2. Curved needle: size of 3.5 in
3. Scissors
4. Stainless steel tweezer

Color and Number of Beads

1) Perler beads:

Symbol ID	Color preview	Count
Z		960
Y		180
R		1 380
P		1 800
O		240
M		60
G		780
E		60
C		1 320
B		480
A		360
Skip		~~60~~

2) Ball beads:

Dark Purple		12 ball beads (12 mm) – for 12 holes at joint

Note: The colors presented above and on pictures are not precise to show the colors on the actual product.

Element A: Letter Notation

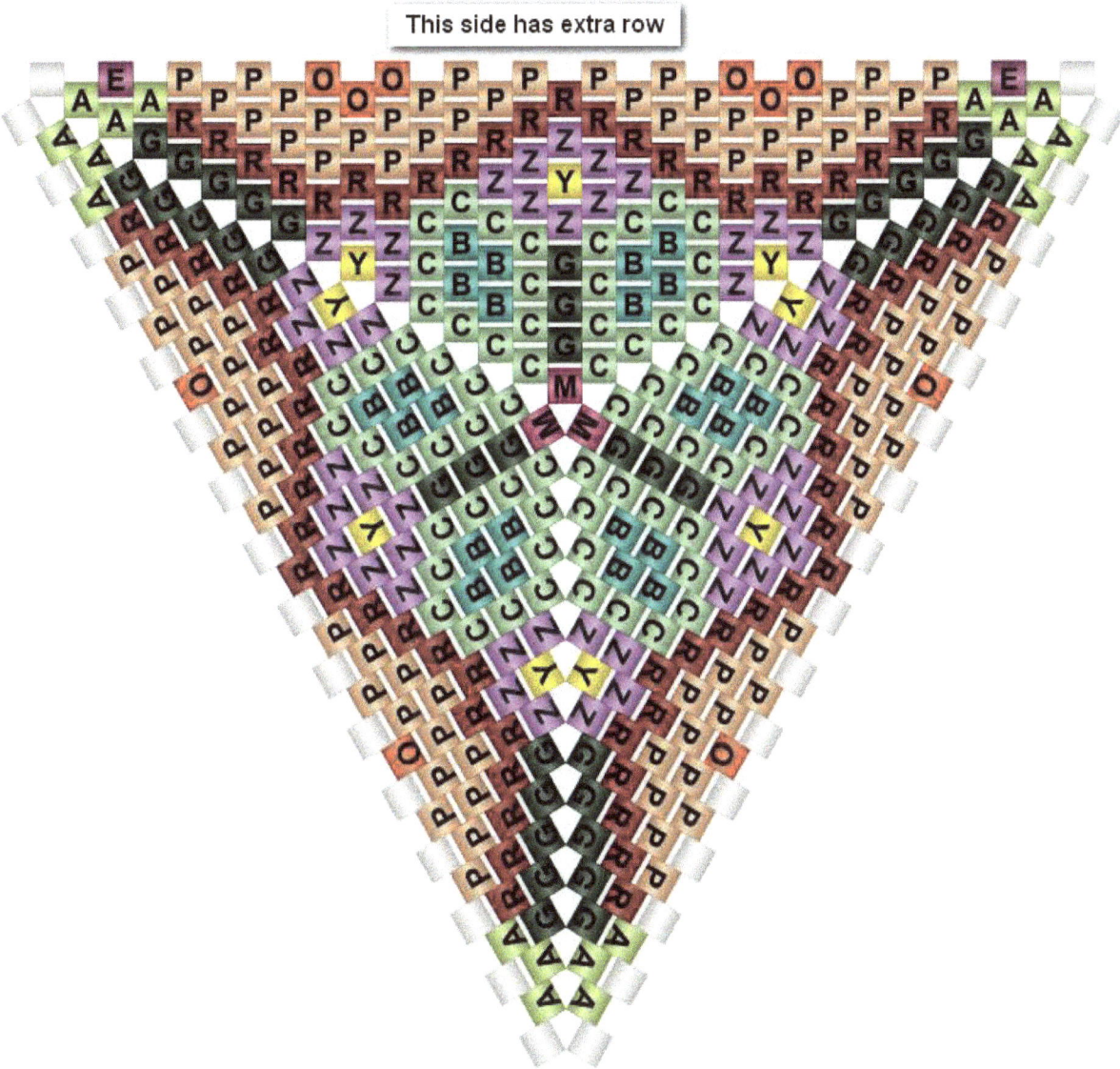

Important: All the white indicators on the graphic are location marking only. There are no beads needed for the places. Please skip all of them by following the element build instruction.

3D Beading Patterns..........33

Element A: Instruction

Total 16 rows

Row 1:   3M.

Row 2:   2C. 2C. 2C.

Row 3:   2C, 1G. 2C, 1G. 2C, 1G.

Row 4:   2C, 1C, 1C. 2C, 1C, 1C. 2C, 1C, 1C.

Row 5:   2C, 1B, 1G, 1B. 2C, 1B, 1G, 1B. 2C, 1B, 1G, 1B.

Row 6:   2Z, 1B, 1C, 1C, 1B. 2Z, 1B, 1C, 1C, 1B. 2Z, 1B, 1C, 1C, 1B.

Row 7:   2Y, 1C, 1B, 1G, 1B, 1C. 2Y, 1C, 1B, 1G, 1B, 1C. 2Y, 1C, 1B, 1G, 1B, 1C.

Row 8:   2Z, 1Z, 1B, 1C, 1C, 1B, 1Z. 2Z, 1Z, 1B, 1C, 1C, 1B, 1Z. 2Z, 1Z, 1B, 1C, 1C, 1B, 1Z.

Row 9:   2G, 1Z, 1C, 1C, 1Z, 1C, 1C, 1Z. 2G, 1Z, 1C, 1C, 1Z, 1C, 1C, 1Z.
2G, 1Z, 1C, 1C, 1Z, 1C, 1C, 1Z.

Row 10:   2G, 1R, 1R, 1C, 1Z, 1Z, 1C, 1R, 1R. 2G, 1R, 1R, 1C, 1Z, 1Z, 1C, 1R, 1R.
2G, 1R, 1R, 1C, 1Z, 1Z, 1C, 1R, 1R.

Row 11:   2G, 1R, 1R, 1R, 1Z, 1Y, 1Z, 1R, 1R, 1R. 2G, 1R, 1R, 1R, 1Z, 1Y, 1Z, 1R, 1R, 1R.
2G, 1R, 1R, 1R, 1Z, 1Y, 1Z, 1R, 1R, 1R.

Row 12:   2G, 1R, 1P, 1P, 1R, 1Z, 1Z, 1R, 1P, 1P, 1R. 2G, 1R, 1P, 1P, 1R, 1Z, 1Z, 1R, 1P, 1P, 1R.
2G, 1R, 1P, 1P, 1R, 1Z, 1Z, 1R, 1P, 1P, 1R.

Row 13:   2G, 1R, 1P, 1P, 1P, 1R, 1Z, 1R, 1P, 1P, 1P, 1R. 2G, 1R, 1P, 1P, 1P, 1R, 1Z, 1R, 1P, 1P, 1P, 1R.
2G, 1R, 1P, 1P, 1P, 1R, 1Z, 1R, 1P, 1P, 1P, 1R.

Row 14:   2A, 1R, 1P, 1P, 1P, 1P, 1R, 1R, 1P, 1P, 1P, 1P, 1R.
2A, 1R, 1P, 1P, 1P, 1P, 1R, 1R, 1P, 1P, 1P, 1P, 1R.
2A, 1R, 1P, 1P, 1P, 1P, 1R, 1R, 1P, 1P, 1P, 1P, 1R.

Row 15:   2A, 1A, 1P, 1P, 1O, 1P, 1P, 1R, 1P, 1P, 1O, 1P, 1P, 1A.
2A, 1A, 1P, 1P, 1O, 1P, 1P, 1R, 1P, 1P, 1O, 1P, 1P, 1A.
2A, 1A, 1P, 1P, 1O, 1P, 1P, 1R, 1P, 1P, 1O, 1P, 1P, 1A.

The following is the extra row:

Row 16:   Skip, 1E, 1P, 1P, 1O, 1O, 1P, 1P, 1P, 1P, 1O, 1O, 1P, 1P, 1E.

Element A: Number Notation

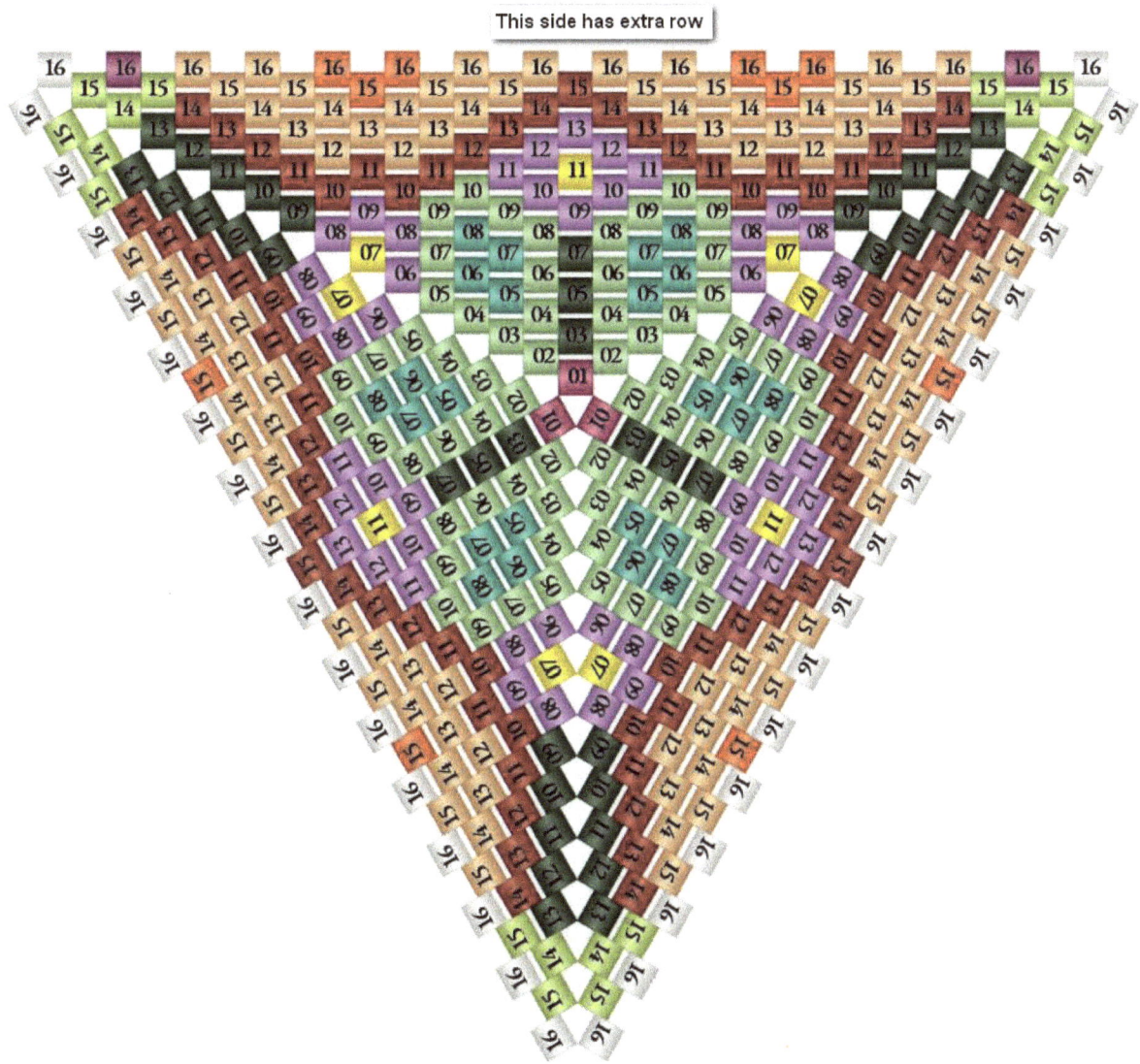

Important: All the white indicators on the graphic are location marking only. There are no beads needed for the places. Please skip all of them by following the element build instruction.

Element B: Letter Notation

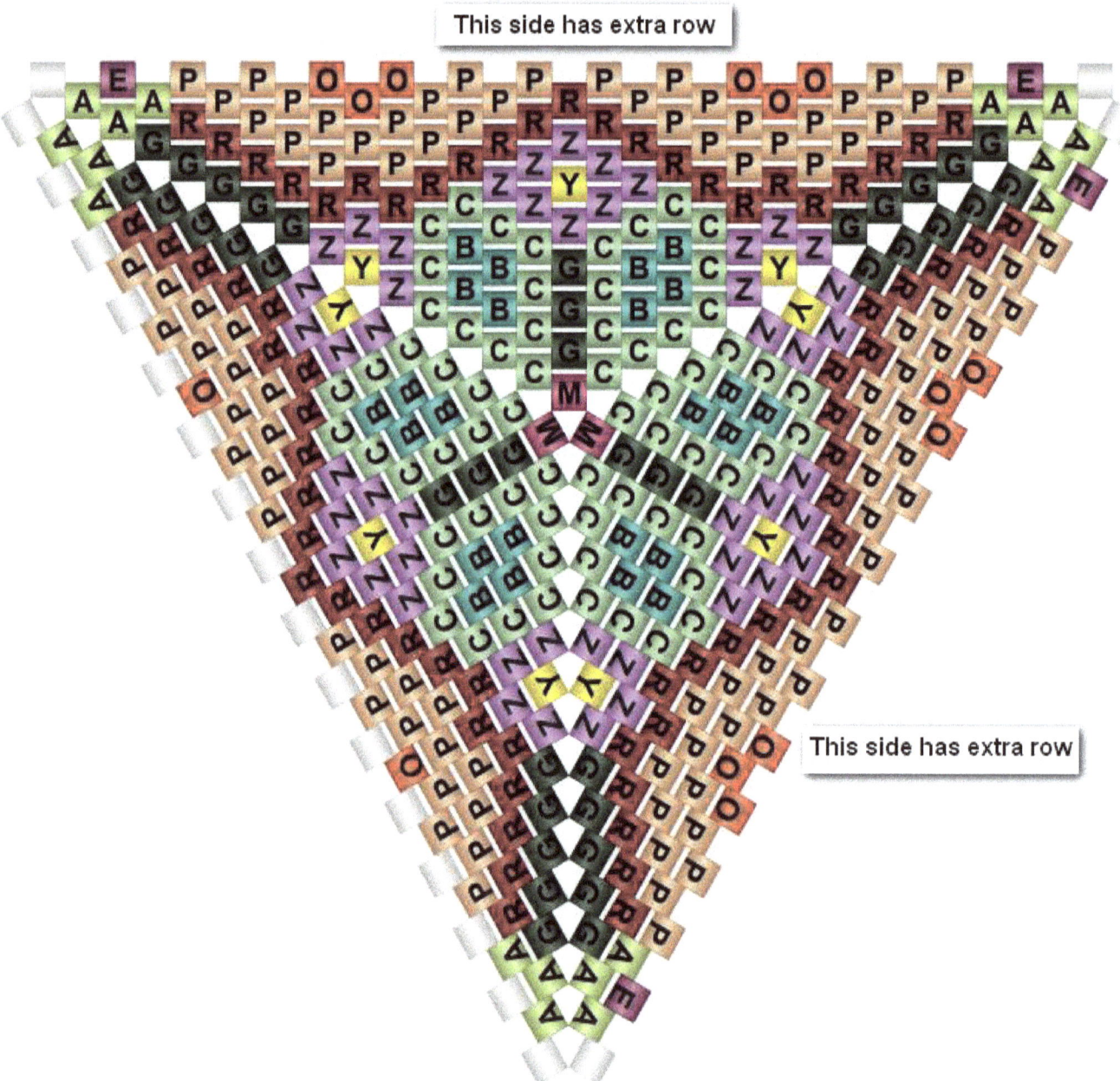

Important: All the white indicators on the graphic are location marking only. There are no beads needed for the places. Please skip all of them by following the element build instruction.

Element B: Instruction

Total 16 rows

Row 1: 3M.

Row 2: 2C. 2C. 2C.

Row 3: 2C, 1G. 2C, 1G. 2C, 1G.

Row 4: 2C, 1C, 1C. 2C, 1C, 1C. 2C, 1C, 1C.

Row 5: 2C, 1B, 1G, 1B. 2C, 1B, 1G, 1B. 2C, 1B, 1G, 1B.

Row 6: 2Z, 1B, 1C, 1C, 1B. 2Z, 1B, 1C, 1C, 1B. 2Z, 1B, 1C, 1C, 1B.

Row 7: 2Y, 1C, 1B, 1G, 1B, 1C. 2Y, 1C, 1B, 1G, 1B, 1C. 2Y, 1C, 1B, 1G, 1B, 1C.

Row 8: 2Z, 1Z, 1B, 1C, 1C, 1B, 1Z. 2Z, 1Z, 1B, 1C, 1C, 1B, 1Z. 2Z, 1Z, 1B, 1C, 1C, 1B, 1Z.

Row 9: 2G, 1Z, 1C, 1C, 1Z, 1C, 1C, 1Z. 2G, 1Z, 1C, 1C, 1Z, 1C, 1C, 1Z.
2G, 1Z, 1C, 1C, 1Z, 1C, 1C, 1Z.

Row 10: 2G, 1R, 1R, 1C, 1Z, 1Z, 1C, 1R, 1R. 2G, 1R, 1R, 1C, 1Z, 1Z, 1C, 1R, 1R.
2G, 1R, 1R, 1C, 1Z, 1Z, 1C, 1R, 1R.

Row 11: 2G, 1R, 1R, 1R, 1Z, 1Y, 1Z, 1R, 1R, 1R. 2G, 1R, 1R, 1R, 1Z, 1Y, 1Z, 1R, 1R, 1R.
2G, 1R, 1R, 1R, 1Z, 1Y, 1Z, 1R, 1R, 1R.

Row 12: 2G, 1R, 1P, 1P, 1R, 1Z, 1Z, 1R, 1P, 1P, 1R. 2G, 1R, 1P, 1P, 1R, 1Z, 1Z, 1R, 1P, 1P, 1R.
2G, 1R, 1P, 1P, 1R, 1Z, 1Z, 1R, 1P, 1P, 1R.

Row 13: 2G, 1R, 1P, 1P, 1P, 1R, 1Z, 1R, 1P, 1P, 1P, 1R. 2G, 1R, 1P, 1P, 1P, 1R, 1Z, 1R, 1P, 1P, 1P, 1R.
2G, 1R, 1P, 1P, 1P, 1R, 1Z, 1R, 1P, 1P, 1P, 1R.

Row 14: 2A, 1R, 1P, 1P, 1P, 1P, 1R, 1R, 1P, 1P, 1P, 1P, 1R.
2A, 1R, 1P, 1P, 1P, 1P, 1R, 1R, 1P, 1P, 1P, 1P, 1R.
2A, 1R, 1P, 1P, 1P, 1P, 1R, 1R, 1P, 1P, 1P, 1P, 1R.

Row 15: 2A, 1A, 1P, 1P, 1O, 1P, 1P, 1R, 1P, 1P, 1O, 1P, 1P, 1A.
2A, 1A, 1P, 1P, 1O, 1P, 1P, 1R, 1P, 1P, 1O, 1P, 1P, 1A.
2A, 1A, 1P, 1P, 1O, 1P, 1P, 1R, 1P, 1P, 1O, 1P, 1P, 1A.

The following is the extra row:

Row 16: Skip, 1E, 1P, 1P, 1O, 1O, 1P, 1P, 1P, 1P, 1O, 1O, 1P, 1P, 1E.
Skip, 1E, 1P, 1P, 1O, 1O, 1P, 1P, 1P, 1P, 1O, 1O, 1P, 1P, 1E.

Element B: Number Notation

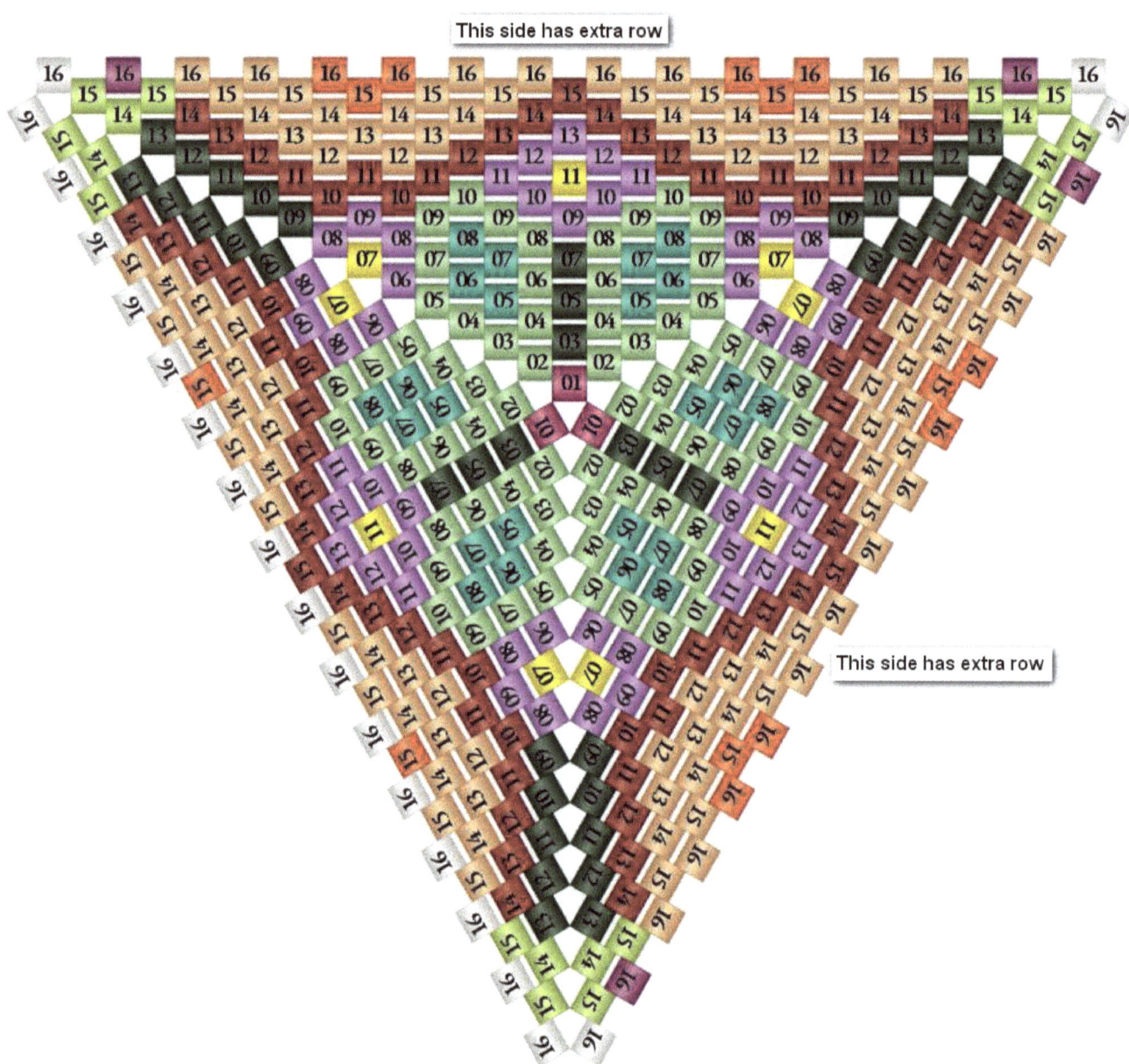

Important: All the white indicators on the graphic are location marking only. There are no beads needed for the places. Please skip all of them by following the element build instruction.

Join Two Triangle Pieces in Zigzag

Note: Please keep the extra string for sewing the ball bead later

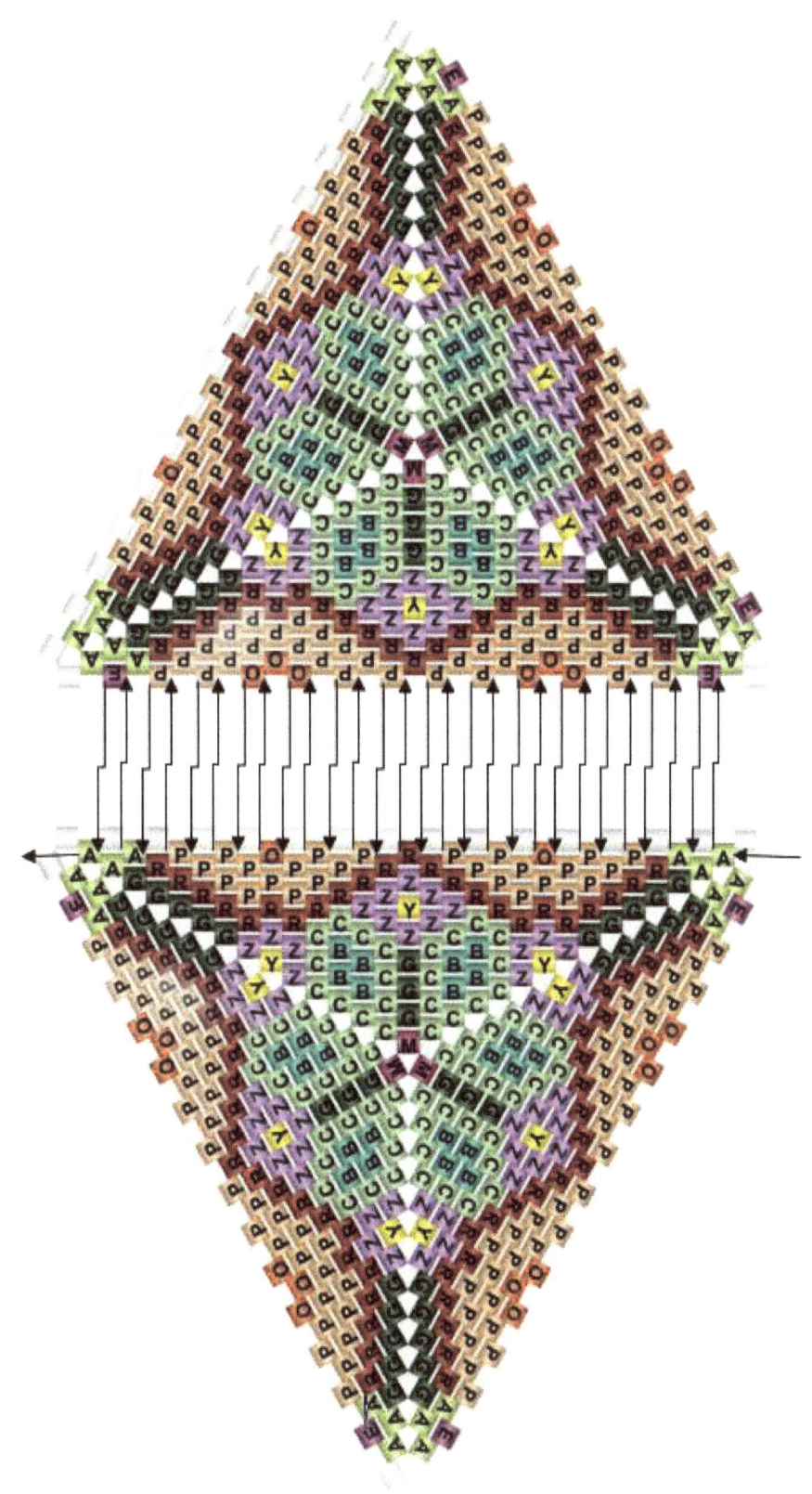

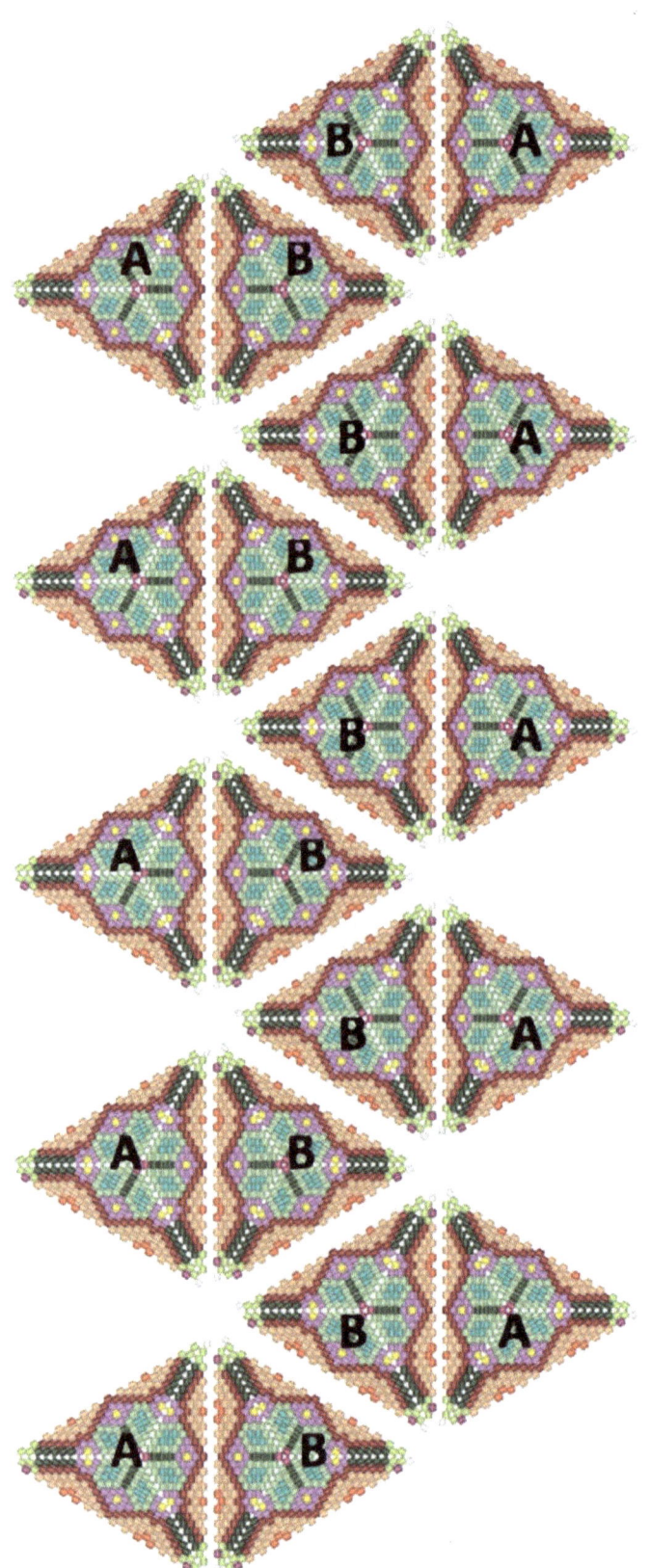

3D Ball – All Piece Demo and Assembling Instruction

Element A:
- 10 pieces
- Please follow Element A instructions to bead. Note each piece has one side with extra row

Element B:
- 10 pieces
- Please follow Element B instructions to bead. Note each piece has two sides with extra row

Assembling:
- Please follow the pattern on the left to sew them together
- Before closing the last piece, fill in the ball with plank foam to keep the ball shape
- After all the 20 triangle pieces are assembled to a ball, sew the 12 mm ball beads to the holes at the joint pointers

Blue Magic

BALL DESCRIPTION:

16 rows, approximately the size of soccer ball, made with 20 pieces of triangles

MATERIALS

1. Perler Beads: 7,620 pieces, 4 colors
2. Ball Beads: 12 pieces, 12 mm in diameter, 1 color
3. Beading String: fishing line – 6 lbs. 160 in for one triangle piece and the ball bead
4. Inside filling: used plank foam

TOOLS

1. Needle: size of 2.5 in
2. Curved needle: size of 3.5 in
3. Scissors
4. Stainless steel tweezer

Color and Number of Beads

3) Perler beads:

Symbol ID	Color preview	Count
R		600
P		3 780
G		60
B		3 180
Skip		~~00~~

4) Ball beads:

Red		12 ball beads (12 mm) – for 12 holes at joint

Note: The colors presented above and on pictures are not precise to show the colors on the actual product.

Element A: Letter Notation

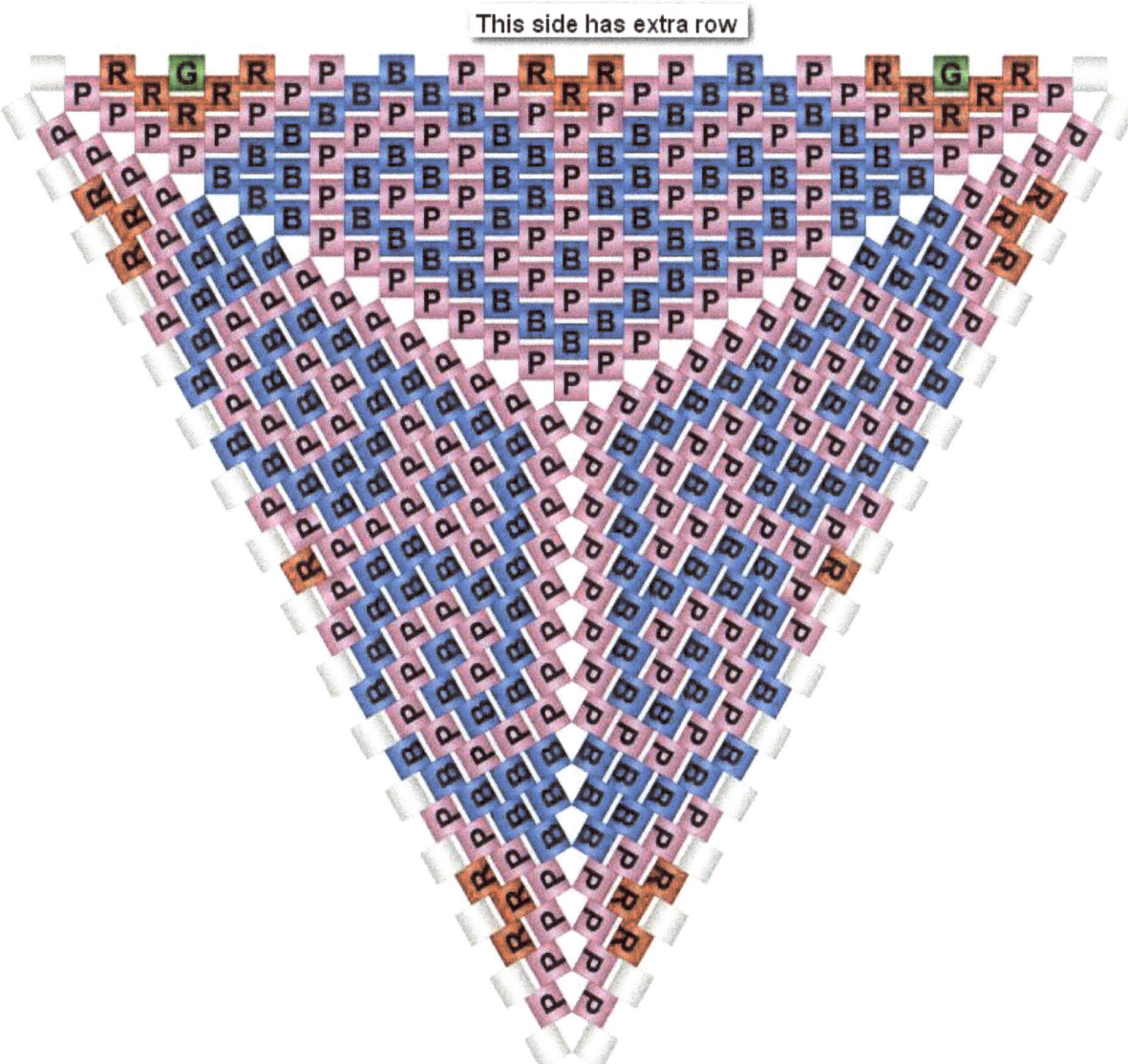

Important: All the white indicators on the graphic are location marking only. There are no beads needed for the places. Please skip all of them by following the element build instruction.

Element A: Instruction
Total 16 rows

Row 1:   3P.

Row 2:   2P, 2P, 2P.

Row 3:   2P, 1B. 2P, 1B. 2P, 1B.

Row 4:   2P, 1B, 1B. 2P, 1B, 1B. 2P, 1B, 1B.

Row 5:   2P, 1B, 1P, 1B. 2P, 1B, 1P, 1B. 2P, 1B, 1P, 1B.

Row 6:   2P, 1B, 1P, 1P, 1B. 2P, 1B, 1P, 1P, 1B. 2P, 1B, 1P, 1P, 1B.

Row 7:   2P, 1B, 1P, 1B, 1P, 1B. 2P, 1B, 1P, 1B, 1P, 1B. 2P, 1B, 1P, 1B, 1P, 1B.

Row 8:   2P, 1B, 1B, 1P, 1P, 1B, 1B. 2P, 1B, 1B, 1P, 1P, 1B, 1B. 2P, 1B, 1B, 1P, 1P, 1B, 1B.

Row 9:   2B, 1B, 1P, 1B, 1P, 1B, 1P, 1B. 2B, 1B, 1P, 1B, 1P, 1B, 1P, 1B. 2B, 1B, 1P, 1B, 1P, 1B, 1P, 1B.

Row 10:   2B, 1P, 1P, 1P, 1B, 1B, 1P, 1P, 1P. 2B, 1P, 1P, 1P, 1B, 1B, 1P, 1P, 1P.
2B, 1P, 1P, 1P, 1B, 1B, 1P, 1P, 1P.

Row 11:   2B, 1B, 1B, 1B, 1B, 1P, 1B, 1B, 1B, 1B. 2B, 1B, 1B, 1B, 1B, 1P, 1B, 1B, 1B, 1B.
2B, 1B, 1B, 1B, 1B, 1P, 1B, 1B, 1B, 1B.

Row 12:   2P, 1B, 1P, 1B, 1P, 1B, 1B, 1P, 1B, 1P, 1B. 2P, 1B, 1P, 1B, 1P, 1B, 1B, 1P, 1B, 1P, 1B.
2P, 1B, 1P, 1B, 1P, 1B, 1B, 1P, 1B, 1P, 1B.

Row 13:   2P, 1P, 1B, 1P, 1P, 1B, 1P, 1B, 1P, 1P, 1B, 1P. 2P, 1P, 1B, 1P, 1P, 1B, 1P, 1B, 1P, 1P, 1B, 1P.
2P, 1P, 1B, 1P, 1P, 1B, 1P, 1B, 1P, 1P, 1B, 1P.

Row 14:   2P, 1R, 1P, 1B, 1P, 1B, 1P, 1P, 1B, 1P, 1B, 1P, 1R.
2P, 1R, 1P, 1B, 1P, 1B, 1P, 1P, 1B, 1P, 1B, 1P, 1R.
2P, 1R, 1P, 1B, 1P, 1B, 1P, 1P, 1B, 1P, 1B, 1P, 1R.

Row 15:   2P, 1R, 1R, 1P, 1B, 1B, 1P, 1R, 1P, 1B, 1B, 1P, 1R, 1R.

The following is the extra row:

Row 16:   Skip, 1R, 1G, 1R, 1P, 1B, 1P, 1R, 1R, 1P, 1B, 1P, 1R, 1G, 1R.

Element A: Number Notation

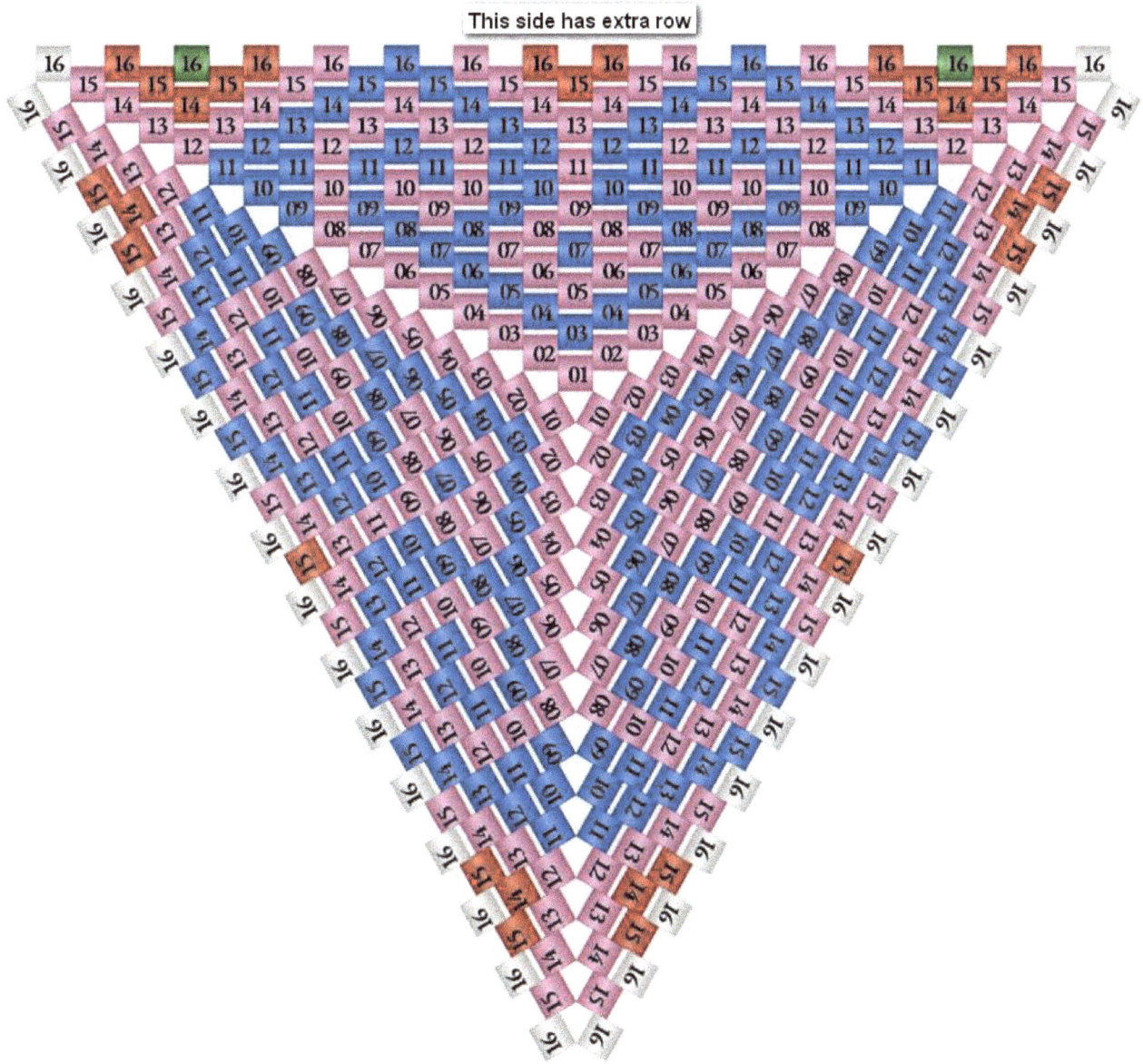

Important: All the white indicators on the graphic are location marking only. There are no beads needed for the places. Please skip all of them by following the element build instruction.

Element B: Letter Notation

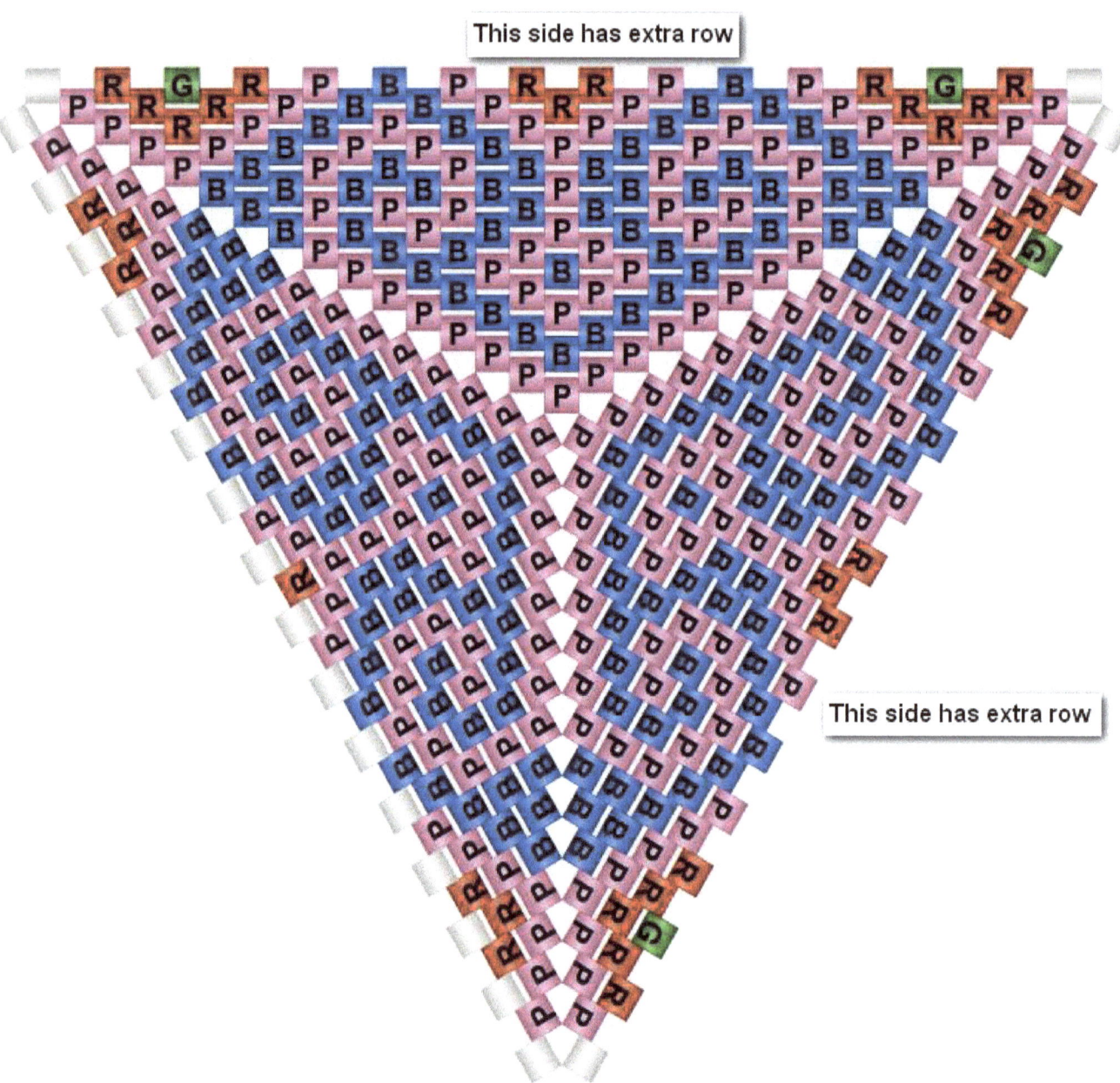

Important: All the white indicators on the graphic are location marking only. There are no beads needed for the places. Please skip all of them by following the element build instruction.

Element B: Instruction

Total 16 rows

Row 1: 3P.

Row 2: 2P, 2P, 2P.

Row 3: 2P, 1B. 2P, 1B. 2P, 1B.

Row 4: 2P, 1B, 1B. 2P, 1B, 1B. 2P, 1B, 1B.

Row 5: 2P, 1B, 1P, 1B. 2P, 1B, 1P, 1B. 2P, 1B, 1P, 1B.

Row 6: 2P, 1B, 1P, 1P, 1B. 2P, 1B, 1P, 1P, 1B. 2P, 1B, 1P, 1P, 1B.

Row 7: 2P, 1B, 1P, 1B, 1P, 1B. 2P, 1B, 1P, 1B, 1P, 1B. 2P, 1B, 1P, 1B, 1P, 1B.

Row 8: 2P, 1B, 1B, 1P, 1P, 1B, 1B. 2P, 1B, 1B, 1P, 1P, 1B, 1B. 2P, 1B, 1B, 1P, 1P, 1B, 1B.

Row 9: 2B, 1B, 1P, 1B, 1P, 1B, 1P, 1B. 2B, 1B, 1P, 1B, 1P, 1B, 1P, 1B. 2B, 1B, 1P, 1B, 1P, 1B, 1P, 1B.

Row 10: 2B, 1P, 1P, 1P, 1B, 1B, 1P, 1P, 1P. 2B, 1P, 1P, 1P, 1B, 1B, 1P, 1P, 1P.
2B, 1P, 1P, 1P, 1B, 1B, 1P, 1P, 1P.

Row 11: 2B, 1B, 1B, 1B, 1B, 1P, 1B, 1B, 1B, 1B. 2B, 1B, 1B, 1B, 1B, 1P, 1B, 1B, 1B, 1B.
2B, 1B, 1B, 1B, 1B, 1P, 1B, 1B, 1B, 1B.

Row 12: 2P, 1B, 1P, 1B, 1P, 1B, 1B, 1P, 1B, 1P, 1B. 2P, 1B, 1P, 1B, 1P, 1B, 1B, 1P, 1B, 1P, 1B.
2P, 1B, 1P, 1B, 1P, 1B, 1B, 1P, 1B, 1P, 1B.

Row 13: 2P, 1P, 1B, 1P, 1P, 1B, 1P, 1B, 1P, 1P, 1B, 1P. 2P, 1P, 1B, 1P, 1P, 1B, 1P, 1B, 1P, 1P, 1B, 1P.
2P, 1P, 1B, 1P, 1P, 1B, 1P, 1B, 1P, 1P, 1B, 1P.

Row 14: 2P, 1R, 1P, 1B, 1P, 1B, 1P, 1P, 1B, 1P, 1B, 1P, 1R.
2P, 1R, 1P, 1B, 1P, 1B, 1P, 1P, 1B, 1P, 1B, 1P, 1R.
2P, 1R, 1P, 1B, 1P, 1B, 1P, 1P, 1B, 1P, 1B, 1P, 1R.

Row 15: 2P, 1R, 1R, 1P, 1B, 1B, 1P, 1R, 1P, 1B, 1B, 1P, 1R, 1R.
2P, 1R, 1R, 1P, 1B, 1B, 1P, 1R, 1P, 1B, 1B, 1P, 1R, 1R.
2P, 1R, 1R, 1P, 1B, 1B, 1P, 1R, 1P, 1B, 1B, 1P, 1R, 1R.

The following is the extra row:

Row 16: Skip, 1R, 1G, 1R, 1P, 1B, 1P, 1R, 1R, 1P, 1B, 1P, 1R, 1G, 1R.
Skip, 1R, 1G, 1R, 1P, 1B, 1P, 1R, 1R, 1P, 1B, 1P, 1R, 1G, 1R.

Element B: Number Notation

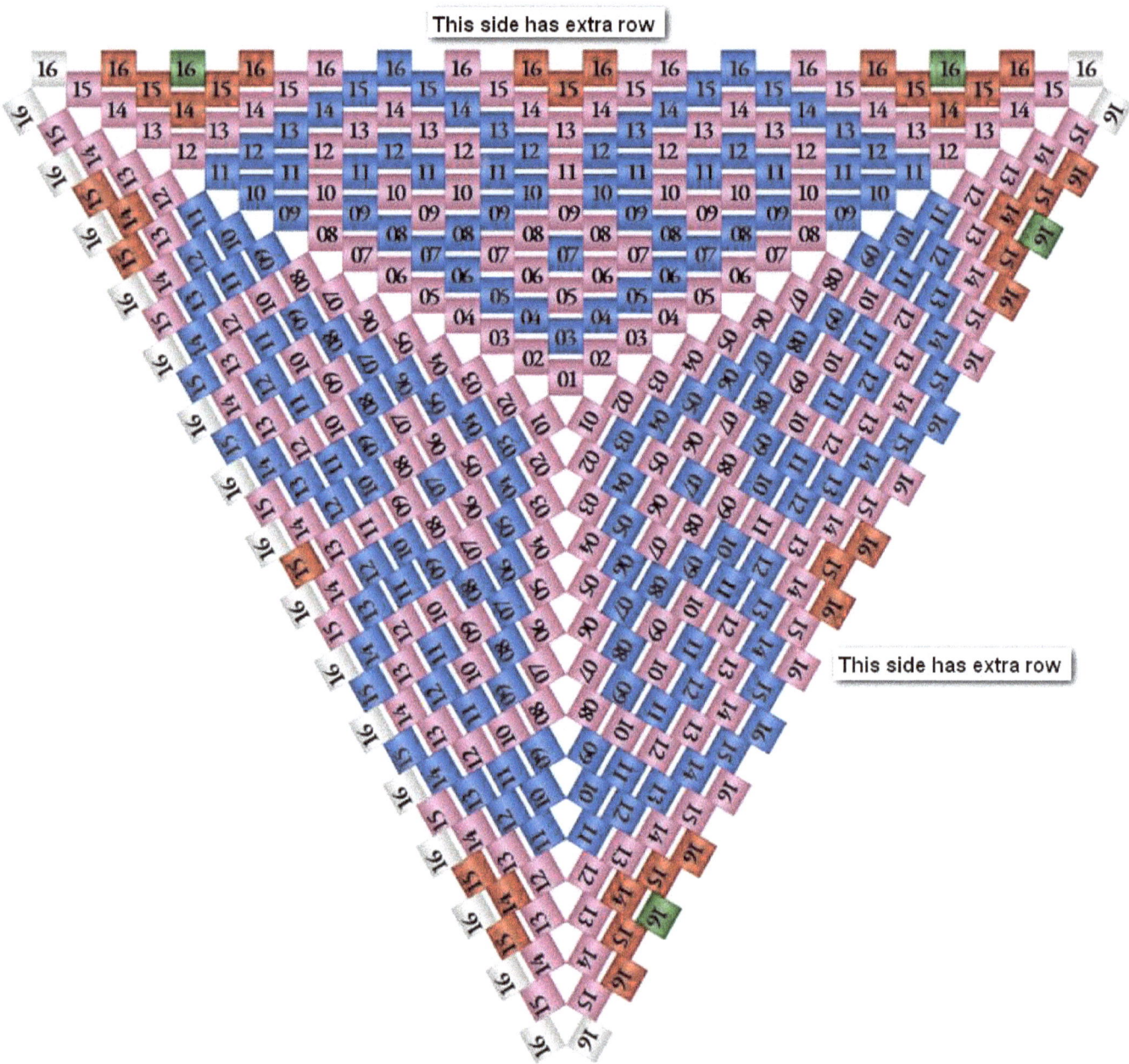

Important: All the white indicators on the graphic are location marking only. There are no beads needed for the places. Please skip all of them by following the element build instruction.

Join Two Triangle Pieces in Zigzag

Note: Please keep the extra string for sewing the ball bead later

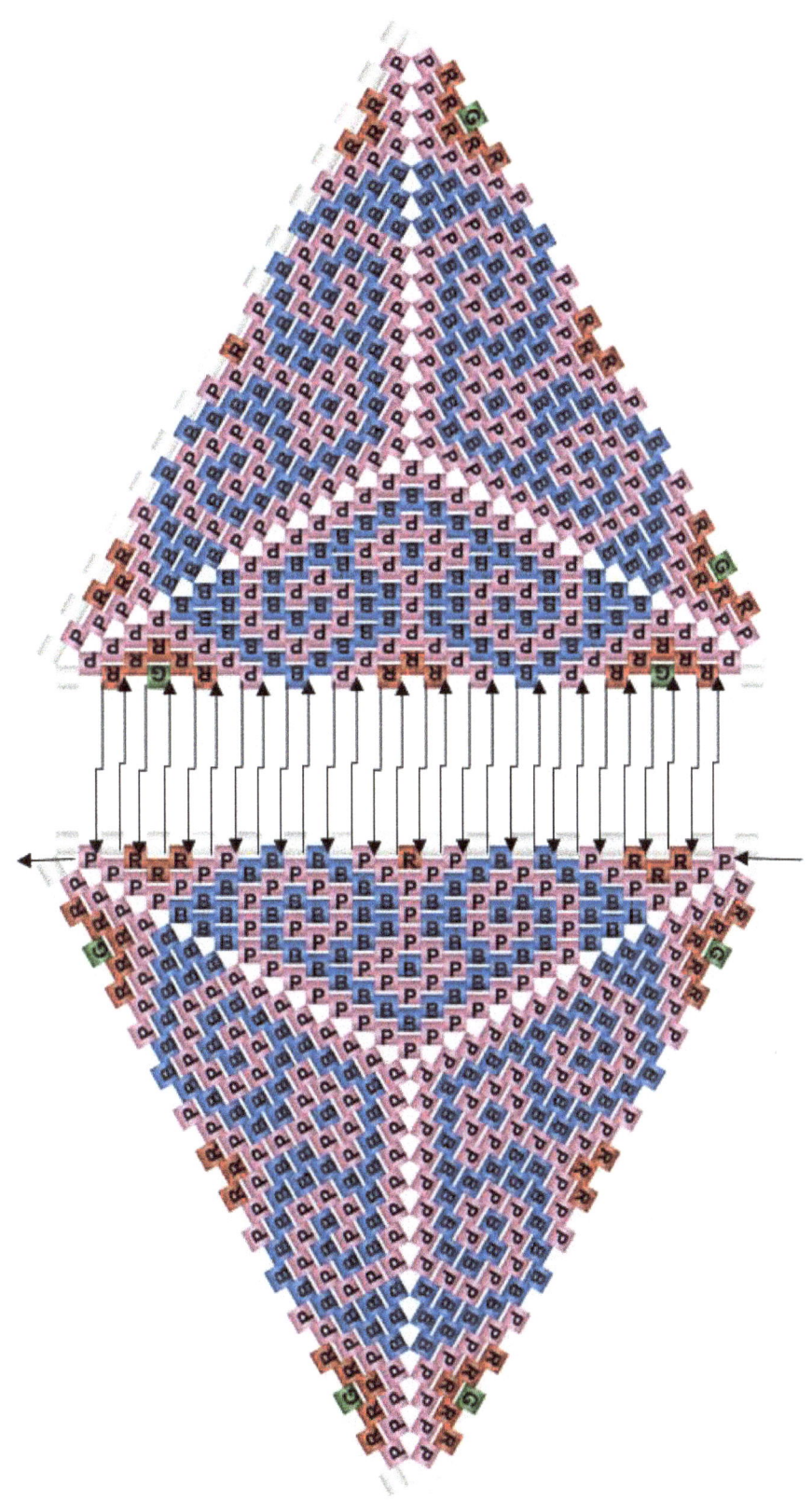

3D Beading Patterns..........49

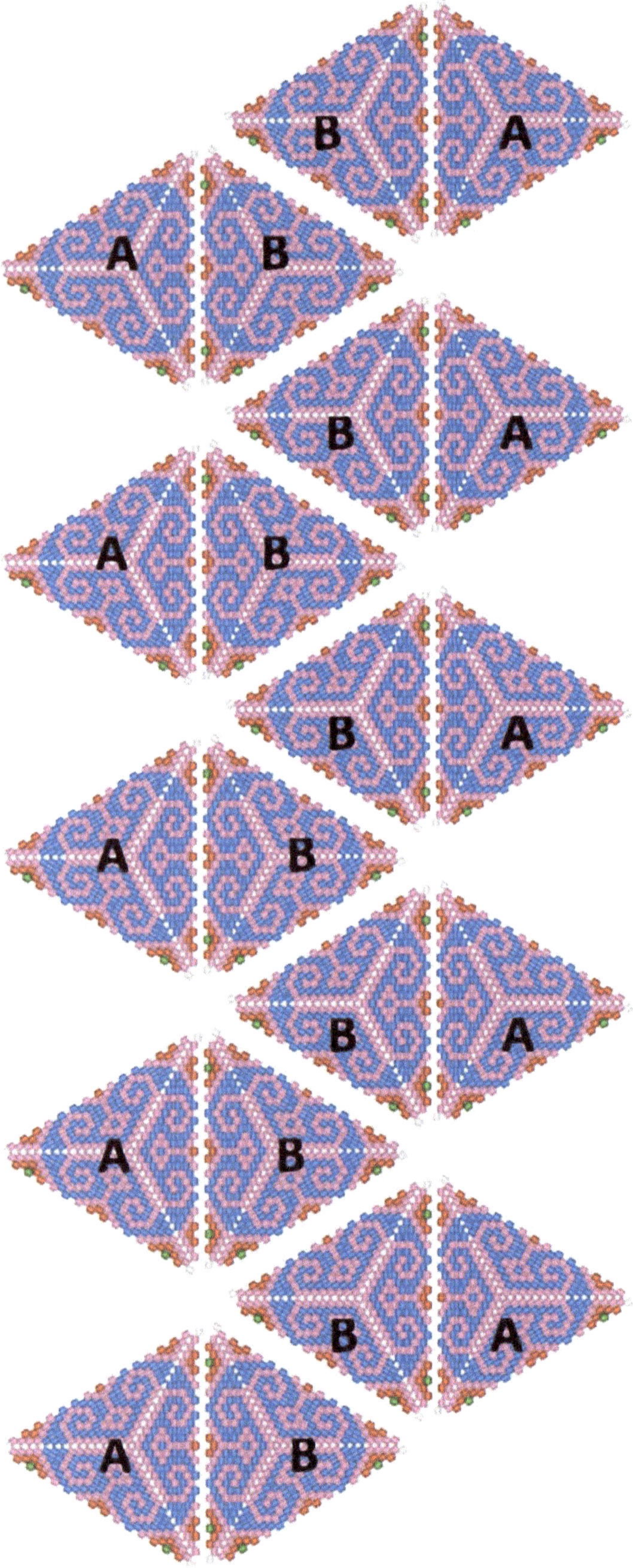

3D Ball – All Piece Demo and Assembling Instruction

Element A:
- 10 pieces
- Please follow Element A instructions to bead. Note each piece has one side with extra row

Element B:
- 10 pieces
- Please follow Element B instructions to bead. Note each piece has two sides with extra row

Assembling:
- Please follow the pattern on the left to sew them together
- Before closing the last piece, fill in the ball with plank foam to keep the ball shape
- After all the 20 triangle pieces are assembled to a ball, sew the 12 mm ball beads to the holes at the joint pointers

Singing Spring

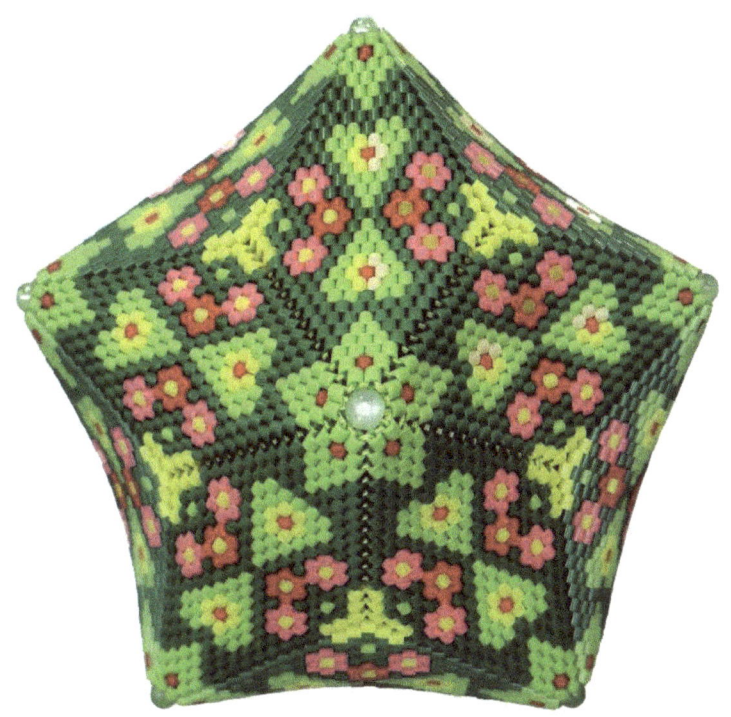

BALL DESCRIPTION:

16 rows, approximately the size of soccer ball, made with 20 pieces of triangles

MATERIALS

1. Perler Beads: 7,620 pieces, 5 colors
2. Ball Beads: 12 pieces, 12 mm in diameter, 1 color
3. Beading String: fishing line – 6 lbs. 160 in for one triangle piece and the ball bead
4. Inside filling: used plank foam

TOOLS

1. Needle: size of 2.5 in
2. Curved needle: size of 3.5 in
3. Scissors
4. Stainless steel tweezer

Color and Number of Beads

5) Perler beads:

Symbol ID	Color preview	Count
Y		840
G		3 600
C		1 980
P		720
R		480
Skip		~~60~~

6) Ball beads:

Sour apple		12 ball beads (12 mm) – for 12 holes at joint

Note: The colors presented above and on pictures are not precise to show the colors on the actual product.

Element A: Letter Notation

Important: All the white indicators on the graphic are location marking only. There are no beads needed for the places. Please skip all of them by following the element build instruction.

3D Beading Patterns..........53

Element A: Instruction
Total 16 rows

Row 1:	3Y.
Row 2:	2Y. 2Y. 2Y.
Row 3:	2Y, 1G. 2Y, 1G. 2Y, 1G.
Row 4:	2G, 1G, 1G. 2G, 1G, 1G. 2G, 1G, 1G.
Row 5:	2G, 1G, 1C, 1G. 2G, 1G, 1C, 1G. 2G, 1G, 1C, 1G.
Row 6:	2G, 1P, 1G, 1G, 1P. 2G, 1P, 1G, 1G, 1P. 2G, 1P, 1G, 1G, 1P.
Row 7:	2G, 1P, 1P, 1G, 1P, 1P. 2G, 1P, 1P, 1G, 1P, 1P. 2G, 1P, 1P, 1G, 1P, 1P.
Row 8:	2G, 1G, 1Y, 1G, 1G, 1Y, 1G. 2G, 1G, 1Y, 1G, 1G, 1Y, 1G. 2G, 1G, 1Y, 1G, 1G, 1Y, 1G.
Row 9:	2G, 1G, 1P, 1P, 1R, 1P, 1P, 1G. 2G, 1G, 1P, 1P, 1R, 1P, 1P, 1G. 2G, 1G, 1P, 1P, 1R, 1P, 1P, 1G.
Row 10:	2G, 1G, 1G, 1P, 1R, 1R, 1P, 1G, 1G. 2G, 1G, 1G, 1P, 1R, 1R, 1P, 1G, 1G.
	2G, 1G, 1G, 1P, 1R, 1R, 1P, 1G, 1G.
Row 11:	2G, 1G, 1C, 1G, 1G, 1Y, 1G, 1G, 1C, 1G. 2G, 1G, 1C, 1G, 1G, 1Y, 1G, 1G, 1C, 1G.
	2G, 1G, 1C, 1G, 1G, 1Y, 1G, 1G, 1C, 1G.
Row 12:	2G, 1G, 1C, 1C, 1G, 1R, 1R, 1G, 1C, 1C, 1G. 2G, 1G, 1C, 1C, 1G, 1R, 1R, 1G, 1C, 1C, 1G.
	2G, 1G, 1C, 1C, 1G, 1R, 1R, 1G, 1C, 1C, 1G.
Row 13:	2C, 1G, 1G, 1C, 1C, 1G, 1R, 1G, 1C, 1C, 1G, 1G.
	2C, 1G, 1G, 1C, 1C, 1G, 1R, 1G, 1C, 1C, 1G, 1G.
	2C, 1G, 1G, 1C, 1C, 1G, 1R, 1G, 1C, 1C, 1G, 1G.
Row 14:	2C, 1C, 1G, 1C, 1Y, 1C, 1G, 1G, 1C, 1Y, 1C, 1G, 1C.
	2C, 1C, 1G, 1C, 1Y, 1C, 1G, 1G, 1C, 1Y, 1C, 1G, 1C.
	2C, 1C, 1G, 1C, 1Y, 1C, 1G, 1G, 1C, 1Y, 1C, 1G, 1C.
Row 15:	2C, 1C, 1C, 1G, 1Y, 1Y, 1C, 1G, 1C, 1Y, 1Y, 1G, 1C, 1C.
	2C, 1C, 1C, 1G, 1Y, 1Y, 1C, 1G, 1C, 1Y, 1Y, 1G, 1C, 1C.
	2C, 1C, 1C, 1G, 1Y, 1Y, 1C, 1G, 1C, 1Y, 1Y, 1G, 1C, 1C.

The following is the extra row:

Row 16:	Skip, 1R, 1C, 1C, 1G, 1R, 1C, 1C, 1C, 1C, 1R, 1G, 1C, 1C, 1R.

Element A: Number Notation

Important: All the white indicators on the graphic are location marking only. There are no beads needed for the places. Please skip all of them by following the element build instruction.

Element B: Letter Notation

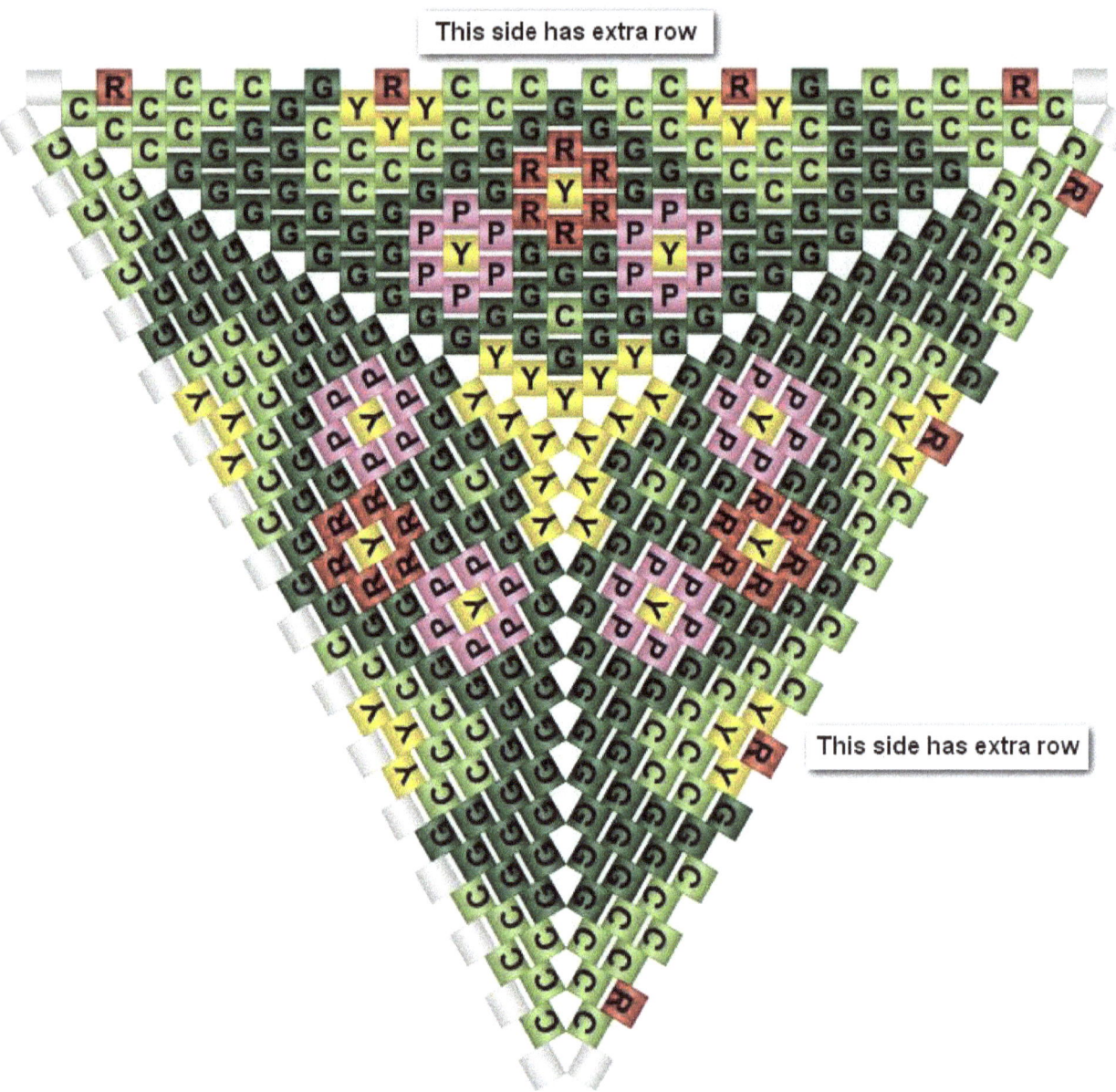

Important: All the white indicators on the graphic are location marking only. There are no beads needed for the places. Please skip all of them by following the element build instruction.

Element B: Instruction

Total 16 rows

Row 1: 3Y.

Row 2: 2Y. 2Y. 2Y.

Row 3: 2Y, 1G. 2Y, 1G. 2Y, 1G.

Row 4: 2G, 1G, 1G. 2G, 1G, 1G. 2G, 1G, 1G.

Row 5: 2G, 1G, 1C, 1G. 2G, 1G, 1C, 1G. 2G, 1G, 1C, 1G.

Row 6: 2G, 1P, 1G, 1G, 1P. 2G, 1P, 1G, 1G, 1P. 2G, 1P, 1G, 1G, 1P.

Row 7: 2G, 1P, 1P, 1G, 1P, 1P. 2G, 1P, 1P, 1G, 1P, 1P. 2G, 1P, 1P, 1G, 1P, 1P.

Row 8: 2G, 1G, 1Y, 1G, 1G, 1Y, 1G. 2G, 1G, 1Y, 1G, 1G, 1Y, 1G. 2G, 1G, 1Y, 1G, 1G, 1Y, 1G.

Row 9: 2G, 1G, 1P, 1P, 1R, 1P, 1P, 1G. 2G, 1G, 1P, 1P, 1R, 1P, 1P, 1G. 2G, 1G, 1P, 1P, 1R, 1P, 1P, 1G.

Row 10: 2G, 1G, 1G, 1P, 1R, 1R, 1P, 1G, 1G. 2G, 1G, 1G, 1P, 1R, 1R, 1P, 1G, 1G.
2G, 1G, 1G, 1P, 1R, 1R, 1P, 1G, 1G.

Row 11: 2G, 1G, 1C, 1G, 1G, 1Y, 1G, 1G, 1C, 1G. 2G, 1G, 1C, 1G, 1G, 1Y, 1G, 1G, 1C, 1G.
2G, 1G, 1C, 1G, 1G, 1Y, 1G, 1G, 1C, 1G.

Row 12: 2G, 1G, 1C, 1C, 1G, 1R, 1R, 1G, 1C, 1C, 1G. 2G, 1G, 1C, 1C, 1G, 1R, 1R, 1G, 1C, 1C, 1G.
2G, 1G, 1C, 1C, 1G, 1R, 1R, 1G, 1C, 1C, 1G.

Row 13: 2C, 1G, 1G, 1C, 1C, 1G, 1R, 1G, 1C, 1C, 1G, 1G.
2C, 1G, 1G, 1C, 1C, 1G, 1R, 1G, 1C, 1C, 1G, 1G.
2C, 1G, 1G, 1C, 1C, 1G, 1R, 1G, 1C, 1C, 1G, 1G.

Row 14: 2C, 1C, 1G, 1C, 1Y, 1C, 1G, 1G, 1C, 1Y, 1C, 1G, 1C.
2C, 1C, 1G, 1C, 1Y, 1C, 1G, 1G, 1C, 1Y, 1C, 1G, 1C.
2C, 1C, 1G, 1C, 1Y, 1C, 1G, 1G, 1C, 1Y, 1C, 1G, 1C.

Row 15: 2C, 1C, 1C, 1G, 1Y, 1Y, 1C, 1G, 1C, 1Y, 1Y, 1G, 1C, 1C.
2C, 1C, 1C, 1G, 1Y, 1Y, 1C, 1G, 1C, 1Y, 1Y, 1G, 1C, 1C.
2C, 1C, 1C, 1G, 1Y, 1Y, 1C, 1G, 1C, 1Y, 1Y, 1G, 1C, 1C.

The following is the extra row:

Row 16: Skip, 1R, 1C, 1C, 1G, 1R, 1C, 1C, 1C, 1C, 1R, 1G, 1C, 1C, 1R.
Skip, 1R, 1C, 1C, 1G, 1R, 1C, 1C, 1C, 1C, 1R, 1G, 1C, 1C, 1R.

Element B: Number Notation

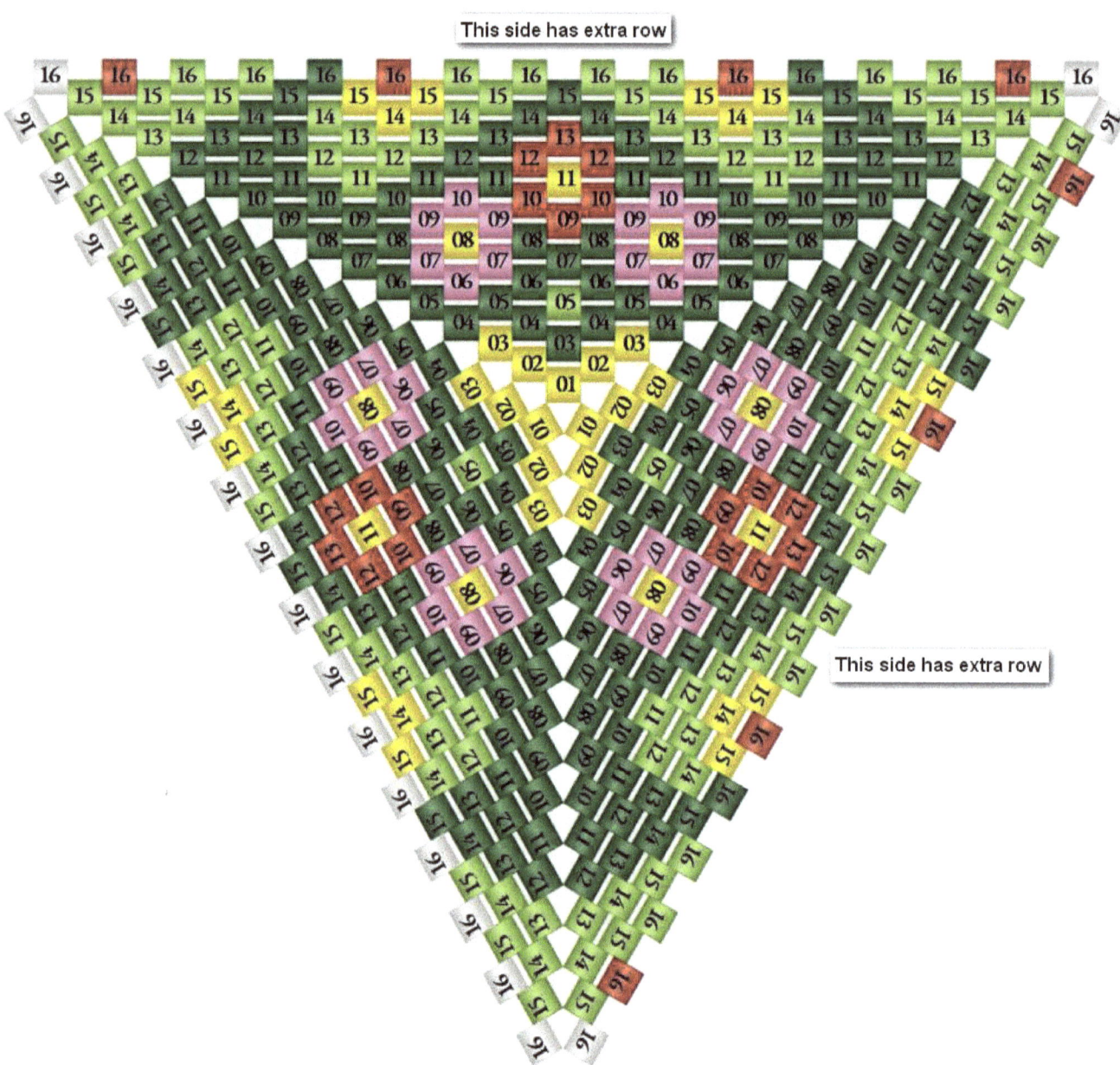

Important: All the white indicators on the graphic are location marking only. There are no beads needed for the places. Please skip all of them by following the element build instruction.

58.........April Days

Join Two Triangle Pieces in Zigzag

Note: Please keep the extra string for sewing the ball bead later

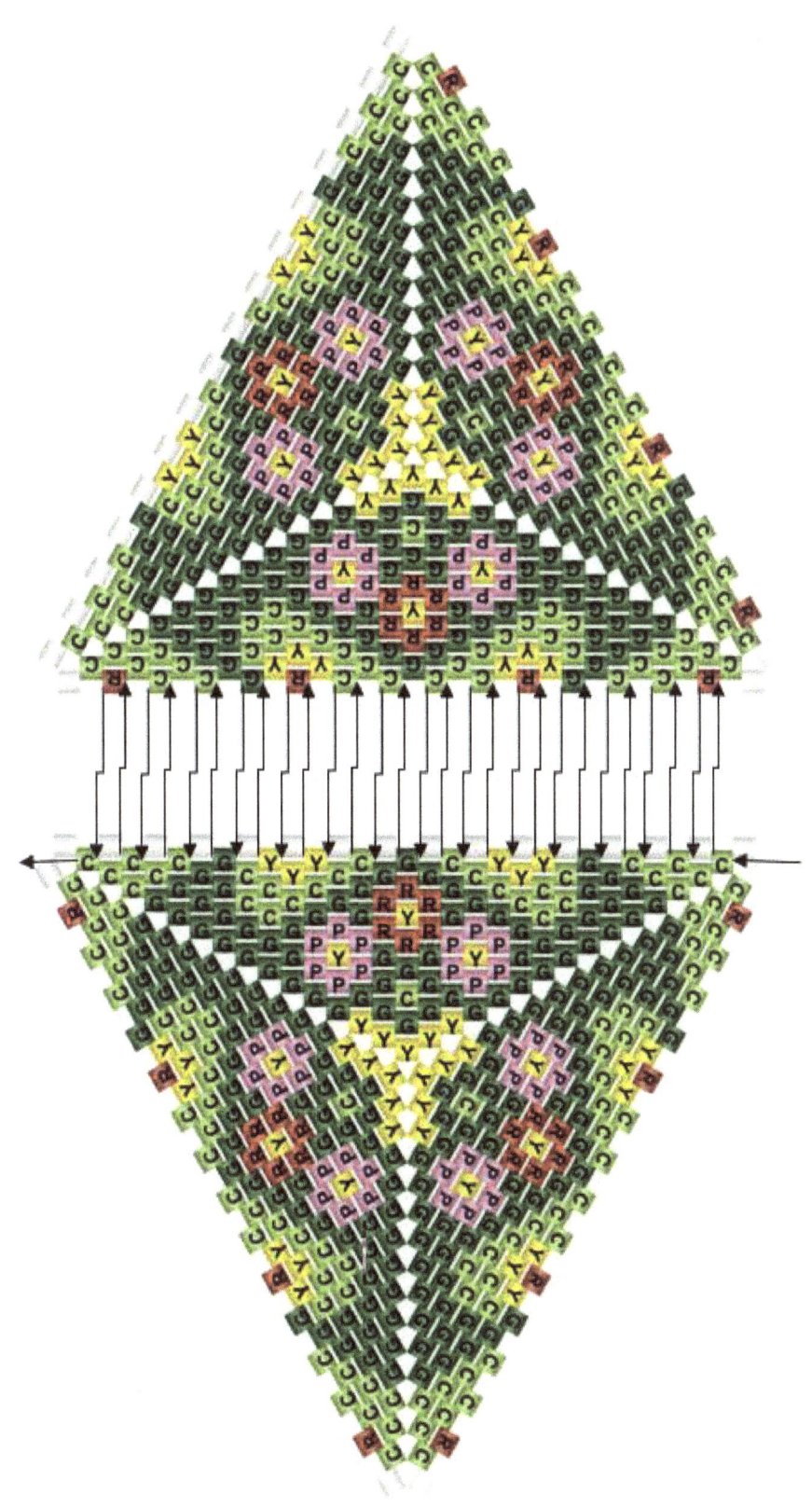

3D Beading Patterns..........59

3D Ball – All Piece Demo and Assembling Instruction

Element A:
- 10 pieces
- Please follow Element A instructions to bead. Note each piece has one side with extra row

Element B:
- 10 pieces
- Please follow Element B instructions to bead. Note each piece has two sides with extra row

Assembling:
- Please follow the pattern on the left to sew them together
- Before closing the last piece, fill in the ball with plank foam to keep the ball shape
- After all the 20 triangle pieces are assembled to a ball, sew the 12 mm ball beads to the holes at the joint pointers

Orange Dream

BALL DESCRIPTION:

16 rows, approximately the size of soccer ball, made with 20 pieces of triangles

MATERIALS

1. Perler Beads: 7,620 pieces, 9 colors
2. Ball Beads: 12 pieces, 12 mm in diameter, 1 color
3. Beading String: fishing line – 6 lbs. 160 in for one triangle piece and the ball bead
4. Inside filling: used plank foam

TOOLS

1. Needle: size of 2.5 in
2. Curved needle: size of 3.5 in
3. Scissors
4. Stainless steel tweezer

Color and Number of Beads

1) Perler beads:

Symbol ID	Color preview	Count
G		120
E		1 680
Z		2 400
O		960
C		780
P		720
B		360
R		480
M		120
Skip		~~60~~

2) Ball beads:

Orange		12 ball beads (12 mm) – for 12 holes at joint

Note: The colors presented above and on pictures are not precise to show the colors on the actual product.

Element A: Letter Notation

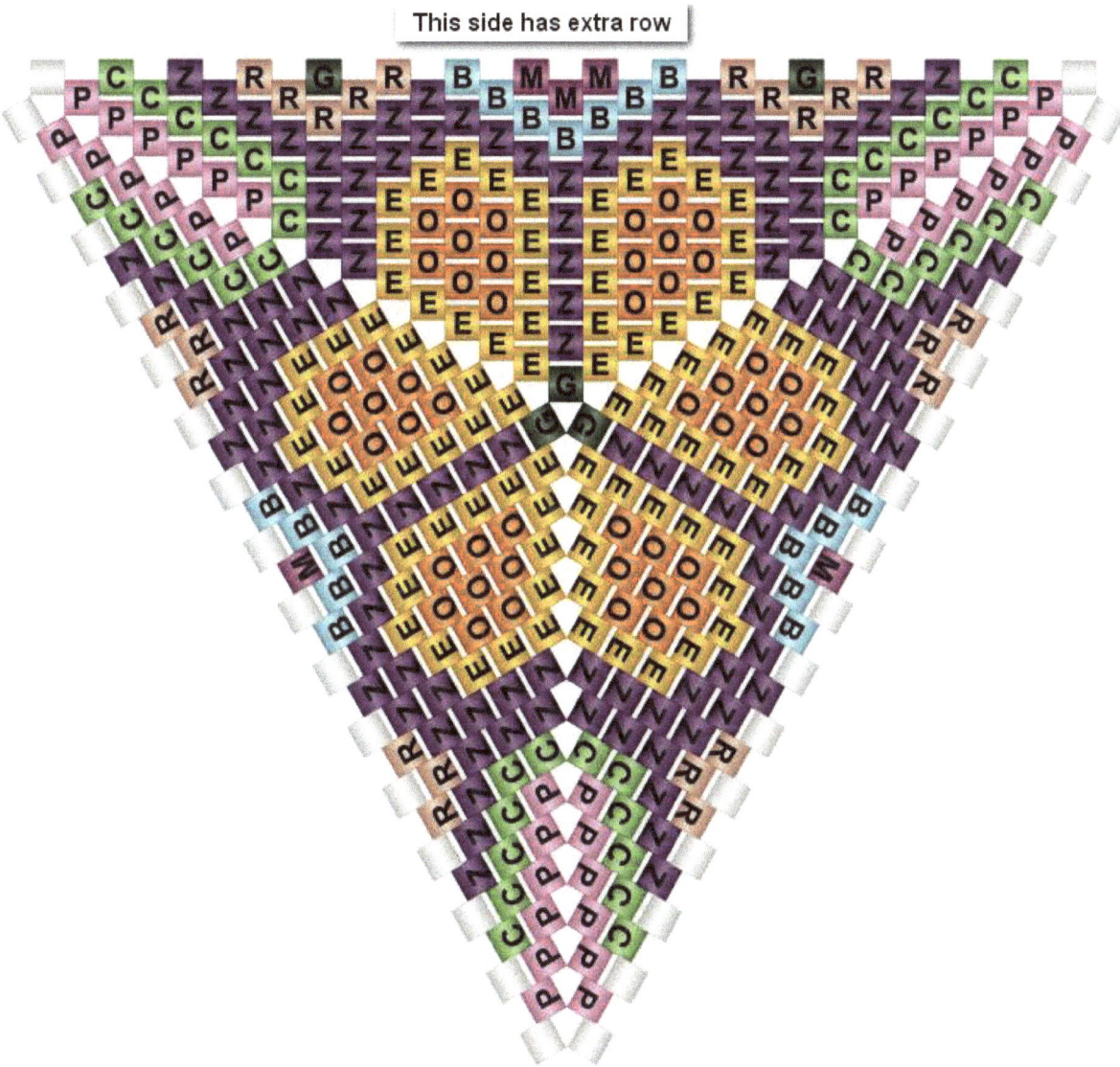

Important: All the white indicators on the graphic are location marking only. There are no beads needed for the places. Please skip all of them by following the element build instruction.

3D Beading Patterns.........63

Element A: Instruction

Total 16 rows

Row 1: 3G.

Row 2: 2E. 2E. 2E.

Row 3: 2E, 1Z. 2E, 1Z. 2E, 1Z.

Row 4: 2E, 1E, 1E. 2E, 1E, 1E. 2E, 1E, 1E.

Row 5: 2E, 1O, 1Z, 1O. 2E, 1O, 1Z, 1O. 2E, 1O, 1Z, 1O.

Row 6: 2E, 1O, 1E, 1E, 1O. 2E, 1O, 1E, 1E, 1O. 2E, 1O, 1E, 1E, 1O.

Row 7: 2Z, 1O, 1O, 1Z, 1O, 1O. 2Z, 1O, 1O, 1Z, 1O, 1O. 2Z, 1O, 1O, 1Z, 1O, 1O.

Row 8: 2Z, 1E, 1O, 1E, 1E, 1O, 1E. 2Z, 1E, 1O, 1E, 1E, 1O, 1E. 2Z, 1E, 1O, 1E, 1E, 1O, 1E.

Row 9: 2C, 1Z, 1O, 1O, 1Z, 1O, 1O, 1Z. 2C, 1Z, 1O, 1O, 1Z, 1O, 1O, 1Z
2C, 1Z, 1O, 1O, 1Z, 1O, 1O, 1Z

Row 10: 2P, 1Z, 1E, 1O, 1E, 1E, 1O, 1E, 1Z. 2P, 1Z, 1E, 1O, 1E, 1E, 1O, 1E, 1Z.
2P, 1Z, 1E, 1O, 1E, 1E, 1O, 1E, 1Z.

Row 11: 2P, 1C, 1Z, 1E, 1E, 1Z, 1E, 1E, 1Z, 1C. 2P, 1C, 1Z, 1E, 1E, 1Z, 1E, 1E, 1Z, 1C.
2P, 1C, 1Z, 1E, 1E, 1Z, 1E, 1E, 1Z, 1C.

Row 12: 2P, 1C, 1Z, 1Z, 1E, 1Z, 1Z, 1E, 1Z, 1Z, 1C. 2P, 1C, 1Z, 1Z, 1E, 1Z, 1Z, 1E, 1Z, 1Z, 1C.
2P, 1C, 1Z, 1Z, 1E, 1Z, 1Z, 1E, 1Z, 1Z, 1C.

Row 13: 2C, 1C, 1Z, 1Z, 1Z, 1Z, 1B, 1Z, 1Z, 1Z, 1Z, 1C. 2C, 1C, 1Z, 1Z, 1Z, 1Z, 1B, 1Z, 1Z, 1Z, 1Z, 1C.
2C, 1C, 1Z, 1Z, 1Z, 1Z, 1B, 1Z, 1Z, 1Z, 1Z, 1C.

Row 14: 2P, 1C, 1Z, 1R, 1Z, 1Z, 1B, 1B, 1Z, 1Z, 1R, 1Z, 1C.
2P, 1C, 1Z, 1R, 1Z, 1Z, 1B, 1B, 1Z, 1Z, 1R, 1Z, 1C.
2P, 1C, 1Z, 1R, 1Z, 1Z, 1B, 1B, 1Z, 1Z, 1R, 1Z, 1C.

Row 15: 2P, 1C, 1Z, 1R, 1R, 1Z, 1B, 1M, 1B, 1Z, 1R, 1R, 1Z, 1C.
2P, 1C, 1Z, 1R, 1R, 1Z, 1B, 1M, 1B, 1Z, 1R, 1R, 1Z, 1C.
2P, 1C, 1Z, 1R, 1R, 1Z, 1B, 1M, 1B, 1Z, 1R, 1R, 1Z, 1C.

The following is the extra row:

Row 16: Skip, 1C, 1Z, 1R, 1G, 1R, 1B, 1M, 1M, 1B, 1R, 1G, 1R, 1Z, 1C.

Element A: Number Notation

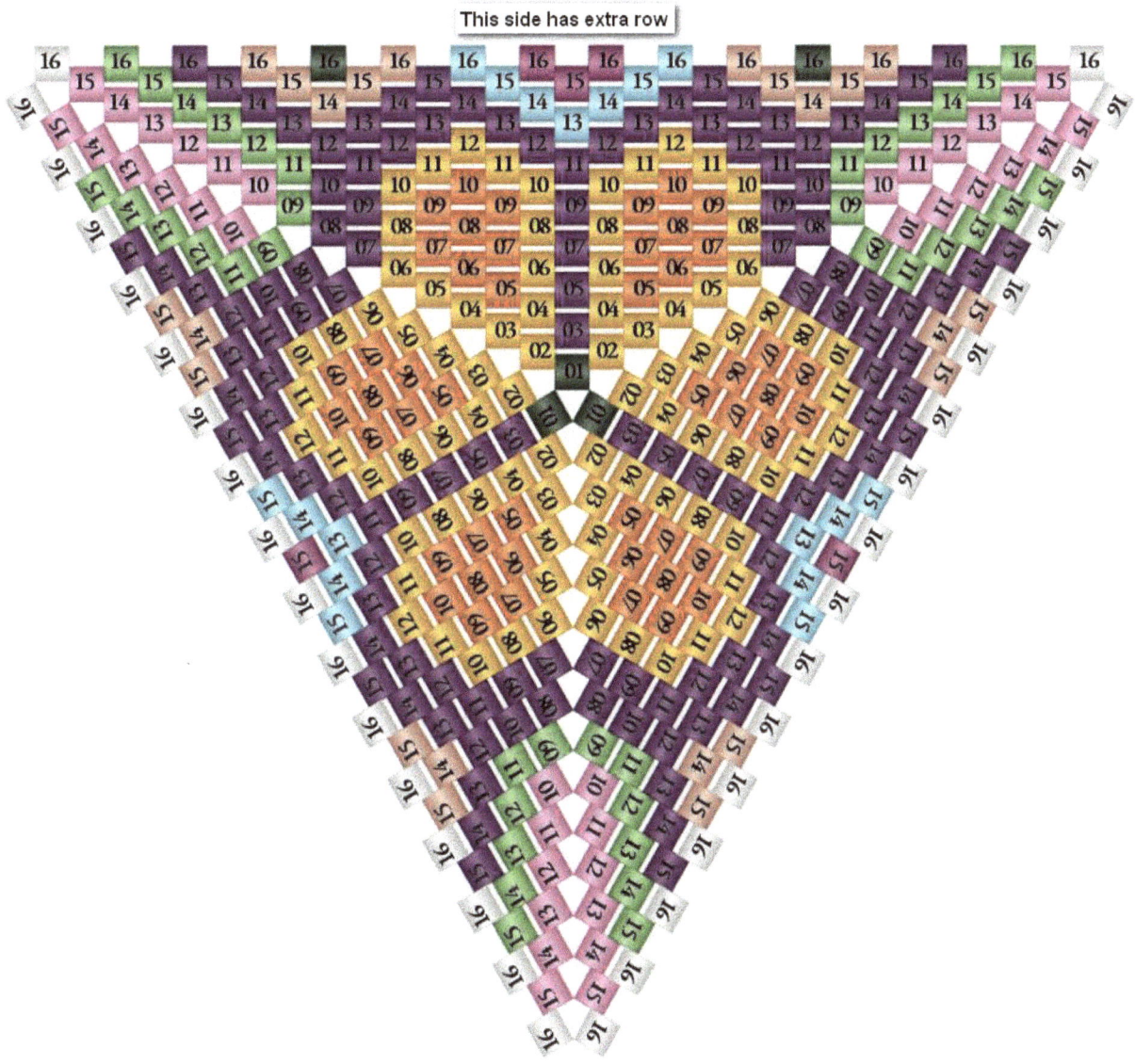

Important: All the white indicators on the graphic are location marking only. There are no beads needed for the places. Please skip all of them by following the element build instruction.

3D Beading Patterns..........65

Element B: Letter Notation

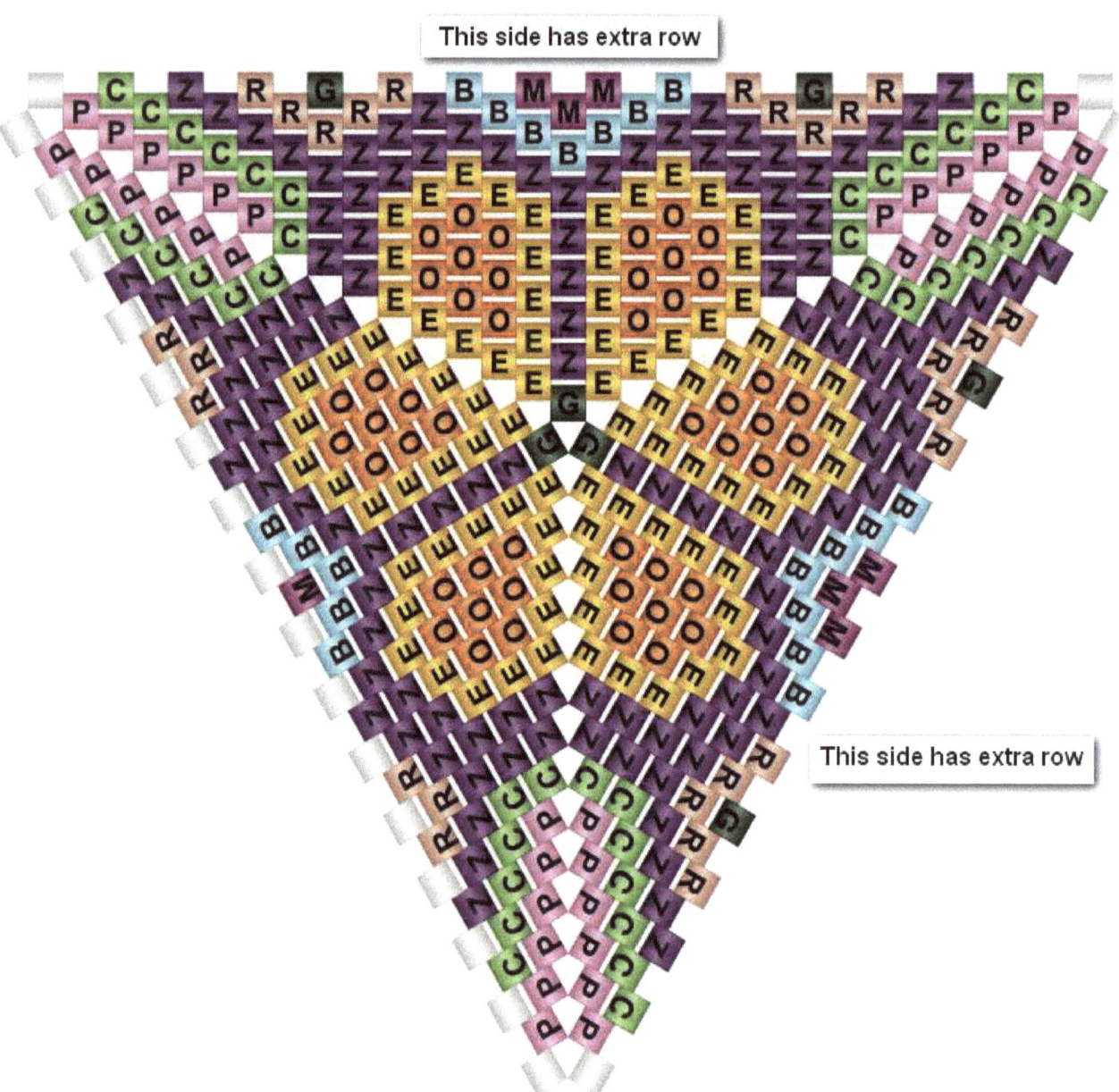

Important: All the white indicators on the graphic are location marking only. There are no beads needed for the places. Please skip all of them by following the element build instruction.

Element B: Instruction
Total 16 rows

Row 1: 3G.

Row 2: 2E. 2E. 2E.

Row 3: 2E, 1Z. 2E, 1Z. 2E, 1Z.

Row 4: 2E, 1E, 1E. 2E, 1E, 1E. 2E, 1E, 1E.

Row 5: 2E, 1O, 1Z, 1O. 2E, 1O, 1Z, 1O. 2E, 1O, 1Z, 1O.

Row 6: 2E, 1O, 1E, 1E, 1O. 2E, 1O, 1E, 1E, 1O. 2E, 1O, 1E, 1E, 1O.

Row 7: 2Z, 1O, 1O, 1Z, 1O, 1O. 2Z, 1O, 1O, 1Z, 1O, 1O. 2Z, 1O, 1O, 1Z, 1O, 1O.

Row 8: 2Z, 1E, 1O, 1E, 1E, 1O, 1E. 2Z, 1E, 1O, 1E, 1E, 1O, 1E. 2Z, 1E, 1O, 1E, 1E, 1O, 1E.

Row 9: 2C, 1Z, 1O, 1O, 1Z, 1O, 1O, 1Z. 2C, 1Z, 1O, 1O, 1Z, 1O, 1O, 1Z
2C, 1Z, 1O, 1O, 1Z, 1O, 1O, 1Z

Row 10: 2P, 1Z, 1E, 1O, 1E, 1E, 1O, 1E, 1Z. 2P, 1Z, 1E, 1O, 1E, 1E, 1O, 1E, 1Z.
2P, 1Z, 1E, 1O, 1E, 1E, 1O, 1E, 1Z.

Row 11: 2P, 1C, 1Z, 1E, 1E, 1Z, 1E, 1E, 1Z, 1C. 2P, 1C, 1Z, 1E, 1E, 1Z, 1E, 1E, 1Z, 1C.
2P, 1C, 1Z, 1E, 1E, 1Z, 1E, 1E, 1Z, 1C.

Row 12: 2P, 1C, 1Z, 1Z, 1E, 1Z, 1Z, 1E, 1Z, 1Z, 1C. 2P, 1C, 1Z, 1Z, 1E, 1Z, 1Z, 1E, 1Z, 1Z, 1C.
2P, 1C, 1Z, 1Z, 1E, 1Z, 1Z, 1E, 1Z, 1Z, 1C.

Row 13: 2C, 1C, 1Z, 1Z, 1Z, 1Z, 1B, 1Z, 1Z, 1Z, 1Z, 1C. 2C, 1C, 1Z, 1Z, 1Z, 1Z, 1B, 1Z, 1Z, 1Z, 1Z, 1C.
2C, 1C, 1Z, 1Z, 1Z, 1Z, 1B, 1Z, 1Z, 1Z, 1Z, 1C.

Row 14: 2P, 1C, 1Z, 1R, 1Z, 1Z, 1B, 1B, 1Z, 1Z, 1R, 1Z, 1C.
2P, 1C, 1Z, 1R, 1Z, 1Z, 1B, 1B, 1Z, 1Z, 1R, 1Z, 1C.
2P, 1C, 1Z, 1R, 1Z, 1Z, 1B, 1B, 1Z, 1Z, 1R, 1Z, 1C.

Row 15: 2P, 1C, 1Z, 1R, 1R, 1Z, 1B, 1M, 1B, 1Z, 1R, 1R, 1Z, 1C.
2P, 1C, 1Z, 1R, 1R, 1Z, 1B, 1M, 1B, 1Z, 1R, 1R, 1Z, 1C.
2P, 1C, 1Z, 1R, 1R, 1Z, 1B, 1M, 1B, 1Z, 1R, 1R, 1Z, 1C.

The following is the extra row:

Row 16: Skip, 1C, 1Z, 1R, 1G, 1R, 1B, 1M, 1M, 1B, 1R, 1G, 1R, 1Z, 1C.
Skip, 1C, 1Z, 1R, 1G, 1R, 1B, 1M, 1M, 1B, 1R, 1G, 1R, 1Z, 1C.

Element B: Number Notation

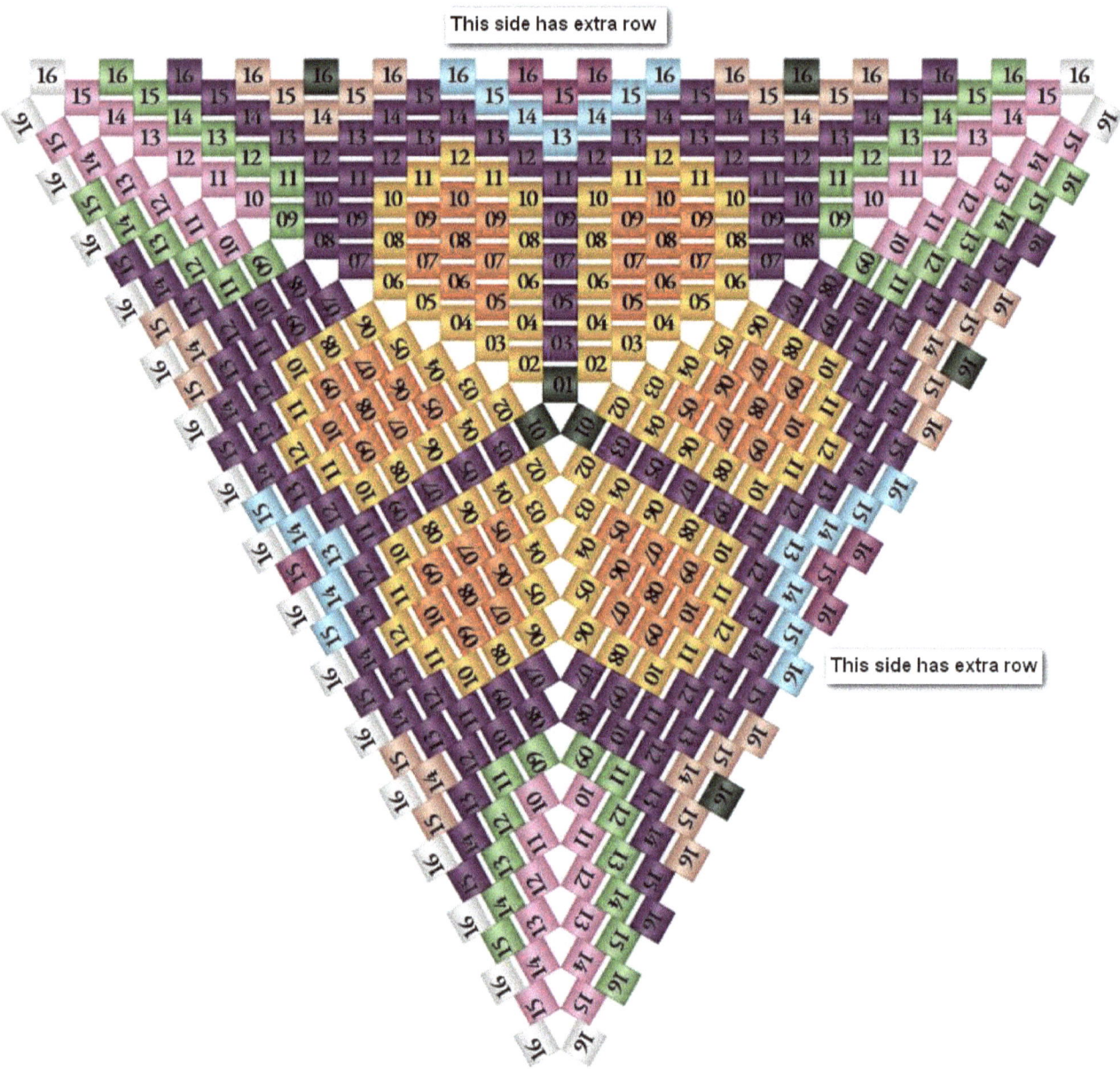

Important: All the white indicators on the graphic are location marking only. There are no beads needed for the places. Please skip all of them by following the element build instruction.

Join Two Triangle Pieces in Zigzag

Note: Please keep the extra string for sewing the ball bead later

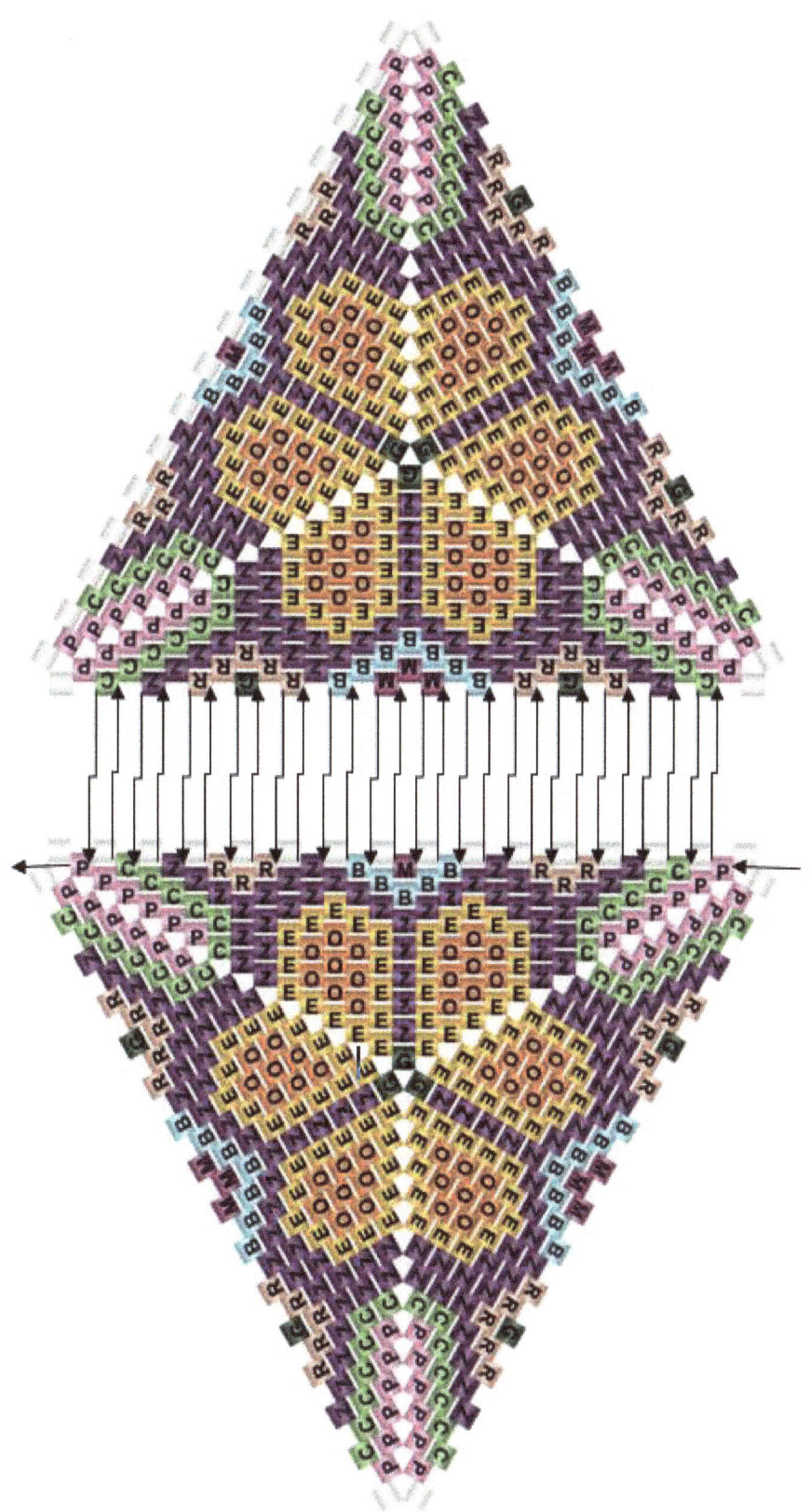

3D Beading Patterns..........69

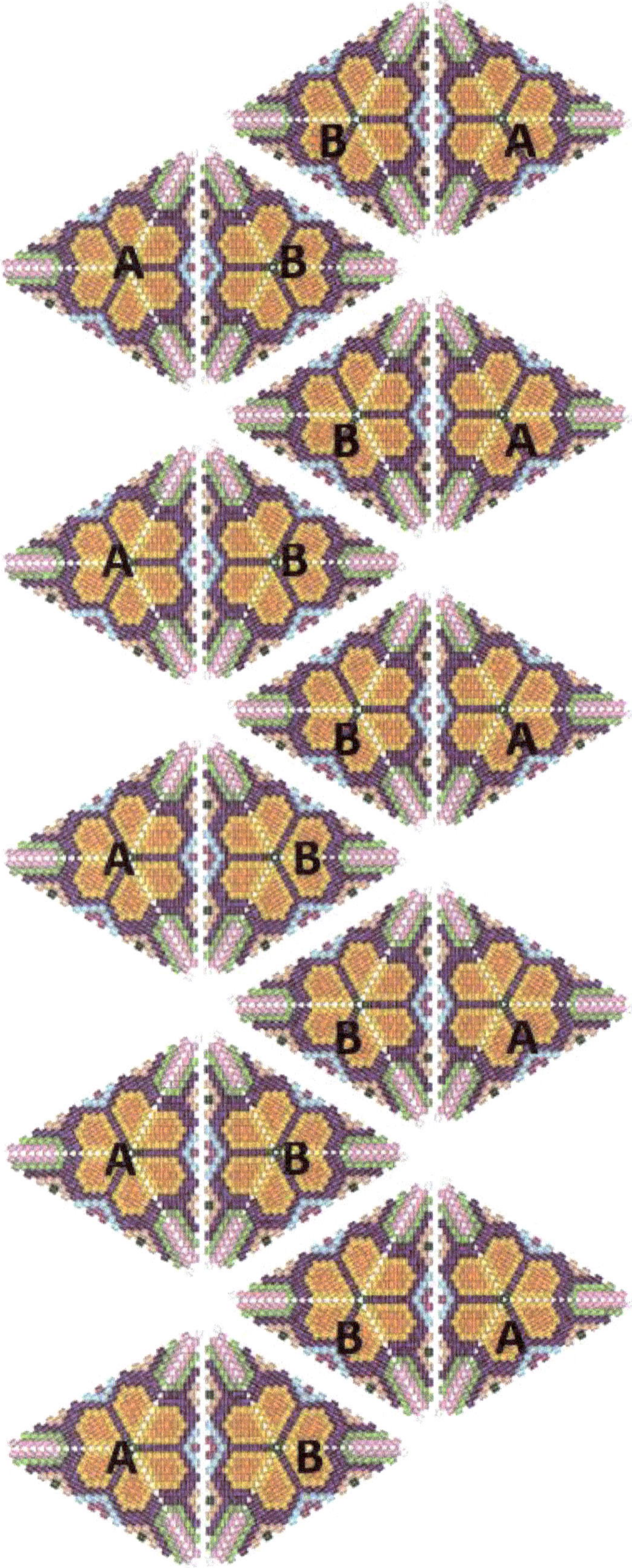

3D Ball – All Piece Demo and Assembling Instruction

Element A:
- 10 pieces
- Please follow Element A instructions to bead. Note each piece has one side with extra row

Element B:
- 10 pieces
- Please follow Element B instructions to bead. Note each piece has two sides with extra row

Assembling:
- Please follow the pattern on the left to sew them together
- Before closing the last piece, fill in the ball with plank foam to keep the ball shape
- After all the 20 triangle pieces are assembled to a ball, sew the 12 mm ball beads to the holes at the joint pointers

Hot Coral

BALL DESCRIPTION:

16 rows, approximately the size of soccer ball, made with 20 pieces of triangles

MATERIALS

1. Perler Beads: 7,620 pieces, 10 colors
2. Ball Beads: 12 pieces, 12 mm in diameter, 1 color
3. Beading String: fishing line – 6 lbs. 160 in for one triangle piece and the ball bead
4. Inside filling: used plank foam

TOOLS

1. Needle: size of 2.5 in
2. Curved needle: size of 3.5 in
3. Scissors
4. Stainless steel tweezer

Color and Number of Beads

1) Perler beads:

Symbol ID	Color preview	Count
Z		600
Y		360
S		60
R		180
P		1 860
O		1 680
H		1 260
F		420
C		600
B		600
Skip		~~00~~

2) Ball beads:

Purple		12 ball beads (12 mm) – for 12 holes at joint

Note: The colors presented above and on pictures are not precise to show the colors on the actual product.

Element A: Letter Notation

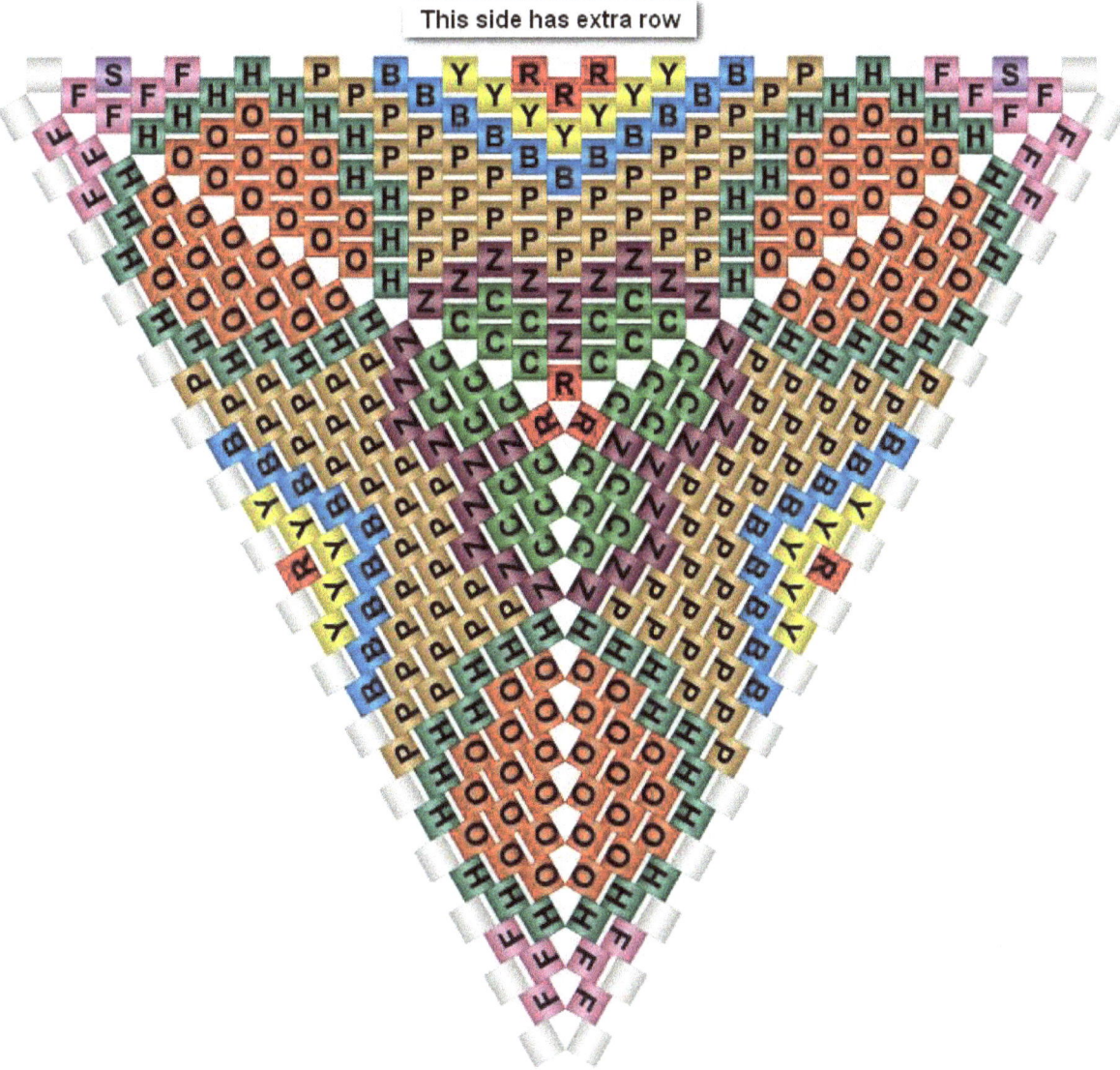

Important: All the white indicators on the graphic are location marking only. There are no beads needed for the places. Please skip all of them by following the element build instruction.

3D Beading Patterns..........73

Element A: Instruction

Total 16 rows

Row 1:   3R

Row 2:   2C. 2C. 2C.

Row 3:   2C, 1Z. 2C, 1Z. 2C, 1Z.

Row 4:   2C, 1C, 1C. 2C, 1C, 1C. 2C, 1C, 1C.

Row 5:   2Z, 1C, 1Z, 1C. 2Z, 1C, 1Z, 1C. 2Z, 1C, 1Z, 1C.

Row 6:   2H, 1Z, 1Z, 1Z, 1Z. 2H, 1Z, 1Z, 1Z, 1Z. 2H, 1Z, 1Z, 1Z, 1Z.

Row 7:   2O, 1P, 1Z, 1P, 1Z, 1P. 2O, 1P, 1Z, 1P, 1Z, 1P. 2O, 1P, 1Z, 1P, 1Z, 1P

Row 8:   2O, 1H, 1P, 1P, 1P, 1P, 1H. 2O, 1H, 1P, 1P, 1P, 1P, 1H. 2O, 1H, 1P, 1P, 1P, 1P, 1H.

Row 9:   2O, 1O, 1P, 1P, 1P, 1P, 1P, 1O. 2O, 1O, 1P, 1P, 1P, 1P, 1P, 1O. 2O, 1O, 1P, 1P, 1P, 1P, 1P, 1O.

Row 10:   2O, 1O, 1H, 1P, 1P, 1P, 1P, 1H, 1O. 2O, 1O, 1H, 1P, 1P, 1P, 1P, 1H, 1O.
2O, 1O, 1H, 1P, 1P, 1P, 1P, 1H, 1O.

Row 11:   2O, 1O, 1H, 1P, 1P, 1B, 1P, 1P, 1H, 1O. 2O, 1O, 1H, 1P, 1P, 1B, 1P, 1P, 1H, 1O.
2O, 1O, 1H, 1P, 1P, 1B, 1P, 1P, 1H, 1O.

Row 12:   2O, 1O, 1O, 1P, 1P, 1B, 1B, 1P, 1P, 1O, 1O. 2O, 1O, 1O, 1P, 1P, 1B, 1B, 1P, 1P, 1O, 1O.
2O, 1O, 1O, 1P, 1P, 1B, 1B, 1P, 1P, 1O, 1O.

Row 13:   2H, 1O, 1O, 1H, 1P, 1B, 1Y, 1B, 1P, 1H, 1O, 1O.
2H, 1O, 1O, 1H, 1P, 1B, 1Y, 1B, 1P, 1H, 1O, 1O.
2H, 1O, 1O, 1H, 1P, 1B, 1Y, 1B, 1P, 1H, 1O, 1O.

Row 14:   2F, 1H, 1O, 1H, 1P, 1B, 1Y, 1Y, 1B, 1P, 1H, 1O, 1H.
2F, 1H, 1O, 1H, 1P, 1B, 1Y, 1Y, 1B, 1P, 1H, 1O, 1H.
2F, 1H, 1O, 1H, 1P, 1B, 1Y, 1Y, 1B, 1P, 1H, 1O, 1H.

Row 15:   2F, 1F, 1H, 1H, 1P, 1B, 1Y, 1R, 1Y, 1B, 1P, 1H, 1H, 1F.
2F, 1F, 1H, 1H, 1P, 1B, 1Y, 1R, 1Y, 1B, 1P, 1H, 1H, 1F.
2F, 1F, 1H, 1H, 1P, 1B, 1Y, 1R, 1Y, 1B, 1P, 1H, 1H, 1F.

The following is the extra row:

Row 16:   Skip, 1S, 1F, 1H, 1P, 1B, 1Y, 1R, 1R, 1Y, 1B, 1P, 1H, 1F, 1S.

Element A: Number Notation

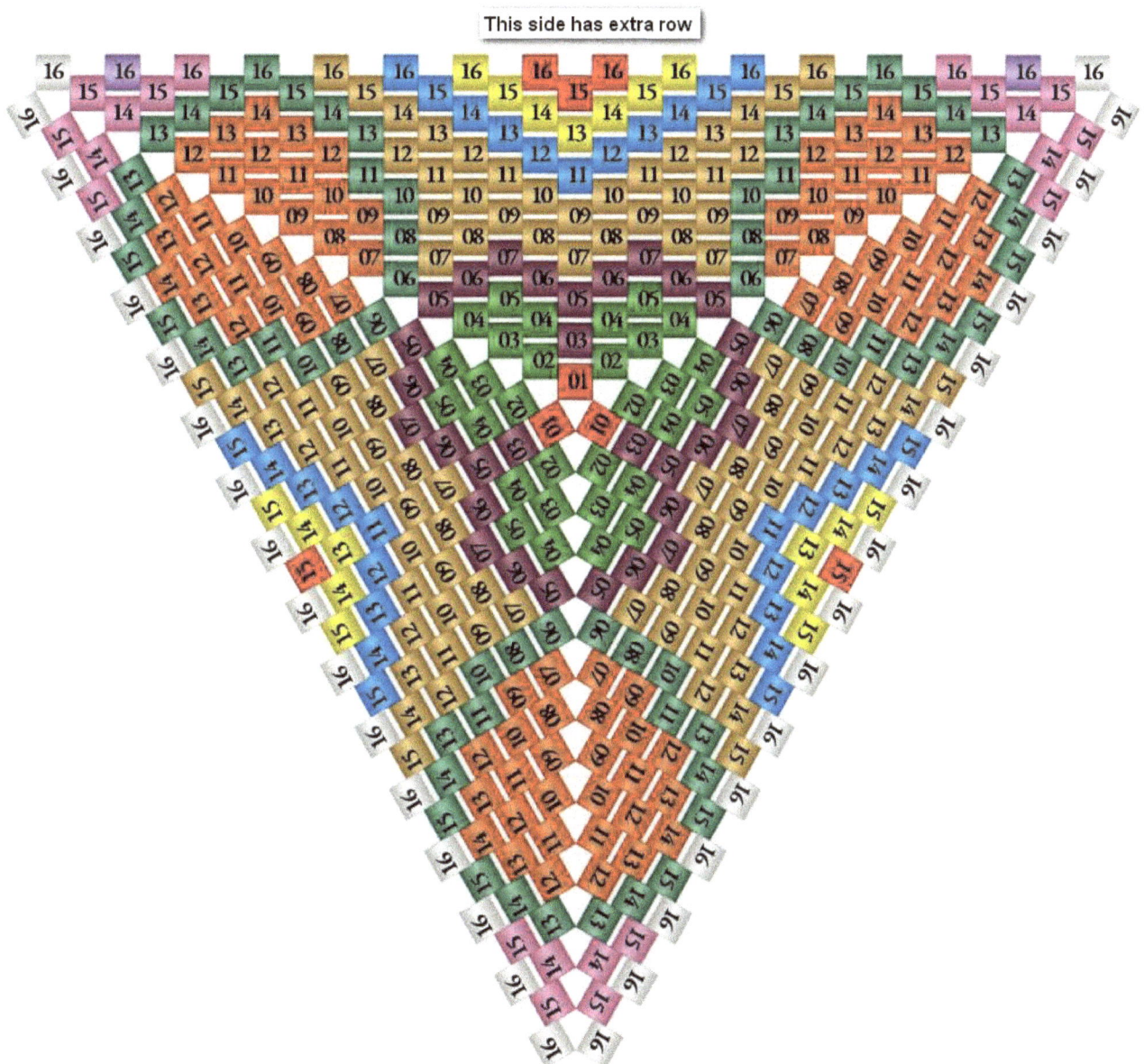

Important: All the white indicators on the graphic are location marking only. There are no beads needed for the places. Please skip all of them by following the element build instruction.

Element B: Letter Notation

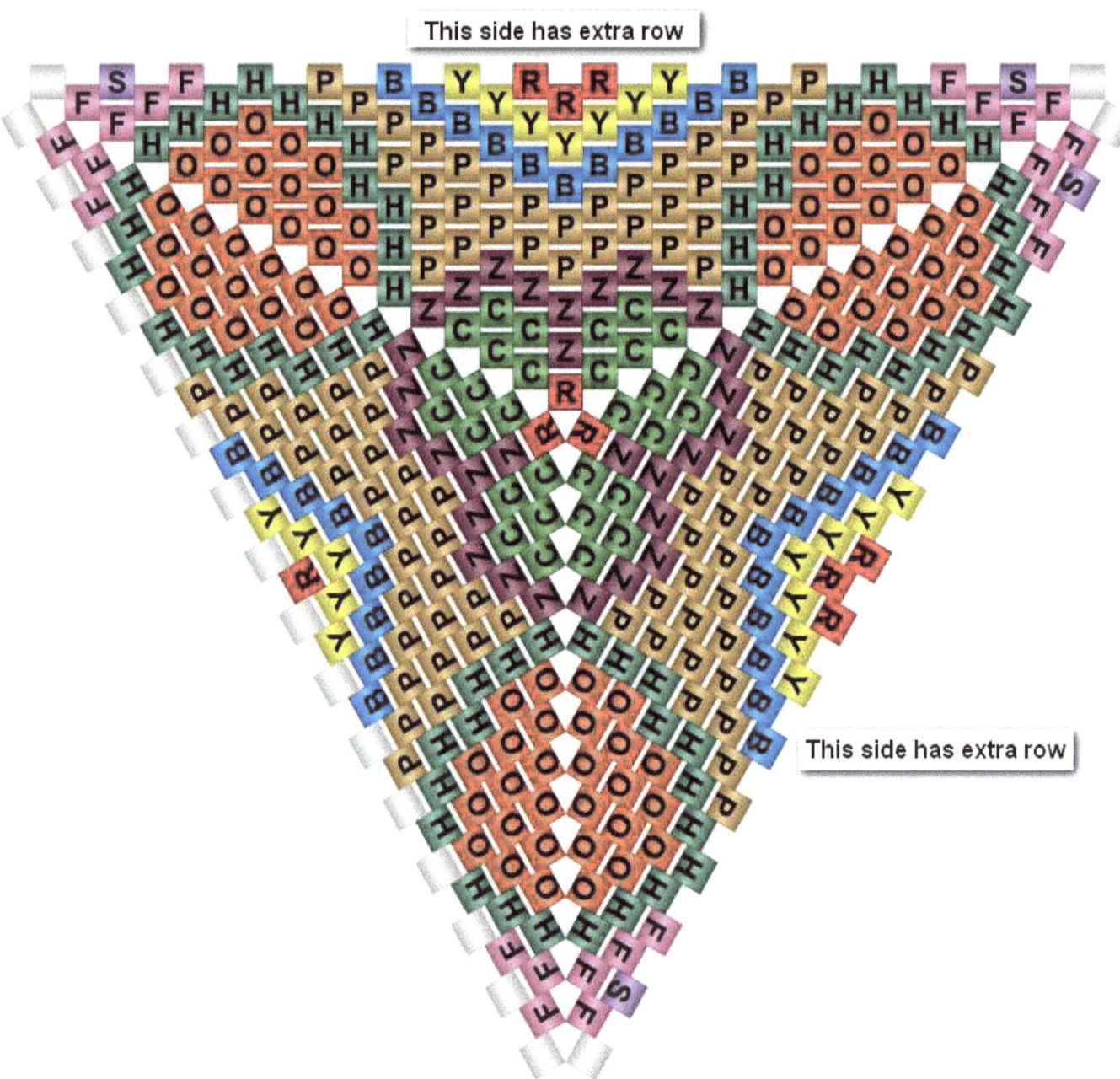

Important: All the white indicators on the graphic are location marking only. There are no beads needed for the places. Please skip all of them by following the element build instruction.

Element B: Instruction

Total 16 rows

Row 1: 3R

Row 2: 2C. 2C. 2C.

Row 3: 2C, 1Z. 2C, 1Z. 2C, 1Z.

Row 4: 2C, 1C, 1C. 2C, 1C, 1C. 2C, 1C, 1C.

Row 5: 2Z, 1C, 1Z, 1C. 2Z, 1C, 1Z, 1C. 2Z, 1C, 1Z, 1C.

Row 6: 2H, 1Z, 1Z, 1Z, 1Z. 2H, 1Z, 1Z, 1Z, 1Z. 2H, 1Z, 1Z, 1Z, 1Z.

Row 7: 2O, 1P, 1Z, 1P, 1Z, 1P. 2O, 1P, 1Z, 1P, 1Z, 1P. 2O, 1P, 1Z, 1P, 1Z, 1P

Row 8: 2O, 1H, 1P, 1P, 1P, 1P, 1H. 2O, 1H, 1P, 1P, 1P, 1P, 1H. 2O, 1H, 1P, 1P, 1P, 1P, 1H.

Row 9: 2O, 1O, 1P, 1P, 1P, 1P, 1P, 1O. 2O, 1O, 1P, 1P, 1P, 1P, 1P, 1O.
2O, 1O, 1P, 1P, 1P, 1P, 1P, 1O.

Row 10: 2O, 1O, 1H, 1P, 1P, 1P, 1P, 1H, 1O. 2O, 1O, 1H, 1P, 1P, 1P, 1P, 1H, 1O.
2O, 1O, 1H, 1P, 1P, 1P, 1P, 1H, 1O.

Row 11: 2O, 1O, 1H, 1P, 1P, 1B, 1P, 1P, 1H, 1O. 2O, 1O, 1H, 1P, 1P, 1B, 1P, 1P, 1H, 1O.
2O, 1O, 1H, 1P, 1P, 1B, 1P, 1P, 1H, 1O.

Row 12: 2O, 1O, 1O, 1P, 1P, 1B, 1B, 1P, 1P, 1O, 1O. 2O, 1O, 1O, 1P, 1P, 1B, 1B, 1P, 1P, 1O, 1O.
2O, 1O, 1O, 1P, 1P, 1B, 1B, 1P, 1P, 1O, 1O.

Row 13: 2H, 1O, 1O, 1H, 1P, 1B, 1Y, 1B, 1P, 1H, 1O, 1O.
2H, 1O, 1O, 1H, 1P, 1B, 1Y, 1B, 1P, 1H, 1O, 1O.
2H, 1O, 1O, 1H, 1P, 1B, 1Y, 1B, 1P, 1H, 1O, 1O.

Row 14: 2F, 1H, 1O, 1H, 1P, 1B, 1Y, 1Y, 1B, 1P, 1H, 1O, 1H.
2F, 1H, 1O, 1H, 1P, 1B, 1Y, 1Y, 1B, 1P, 1H, 1O, 1H.
2F, 1H, 1O, 1H, 1P, 1B, 1Y, 1Y, 1B, 1P, 1H, 1O, 1H.

Row 15: 2F, 1F, 1H, 1H, 1P, 1B, 1Y, 1R, 1Y, 1B, 1P, 1H, 1H, 1F.
2F, 1F, 1H, 1H, 1P, 1B, 1Y, 1R, 1Y, 1B, 1P, 1H, 1H, 1F.
2F, 1F, 1H, 1H, 1P, 1B, 1Y, 1R, 1Y, 1B, 1P, 1H, 1H, 1F.

The following is the extra row:

Row 16: Skip, 1S, 1F, 1H, 1P, 1B, 1Y, 1R, 1R, 1Y, 1B, 1P, 1H, 1F, 1S.
Skip, 1S, 1F, 1H, 1P, 1B, 1Y, 1R, 1R, 1Y, 1B, 1P, 1H, 1F, 1S.

Element B: Number Notation

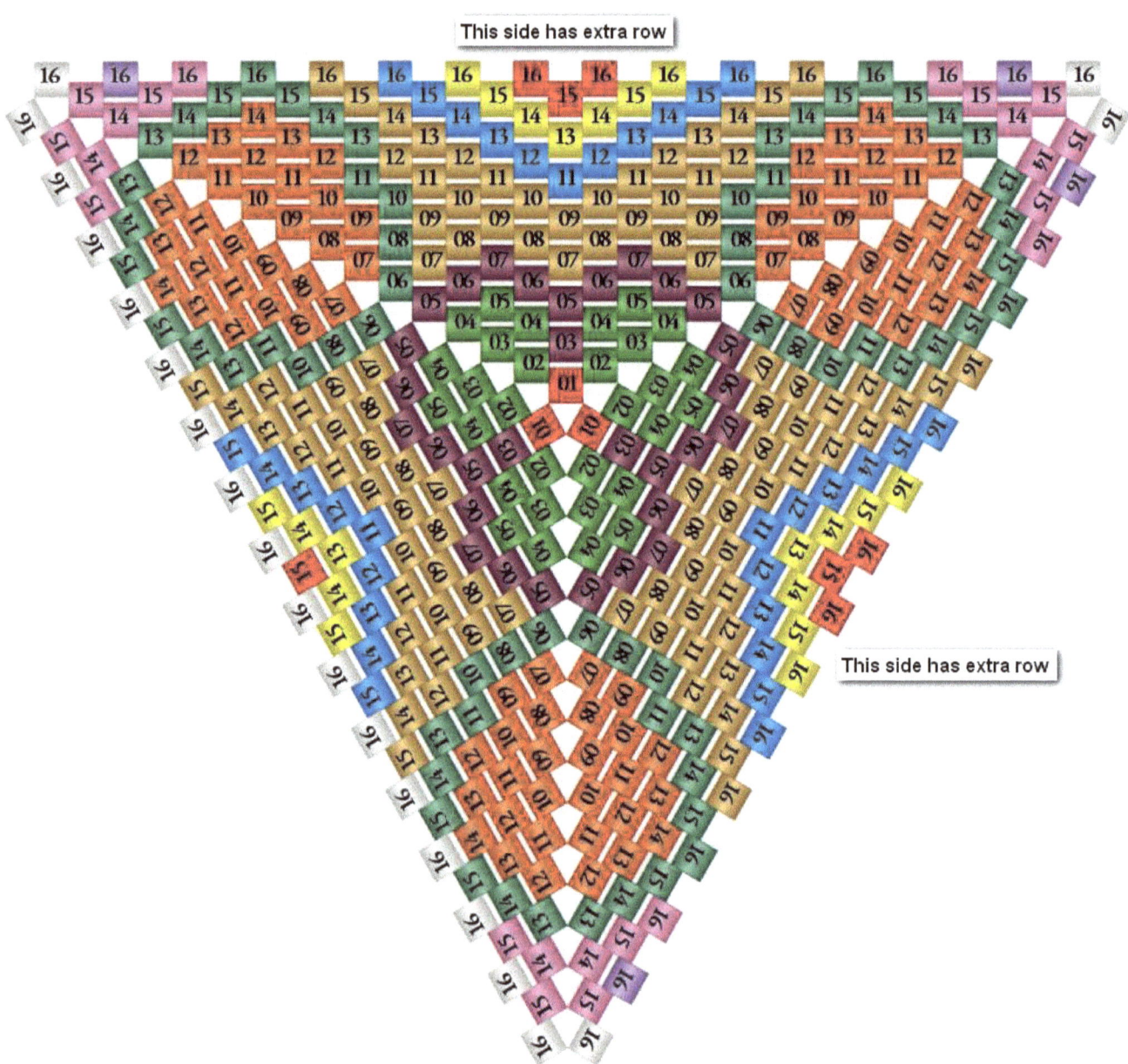

Important: All the white indicators on the graphic are location marking only. There are no beads needed for the places. Please skip all of them by following the element build instruction.

Join Two Triangle Pieces in Zigzag

Note: Please keep the extra string for sewing the ball bead later

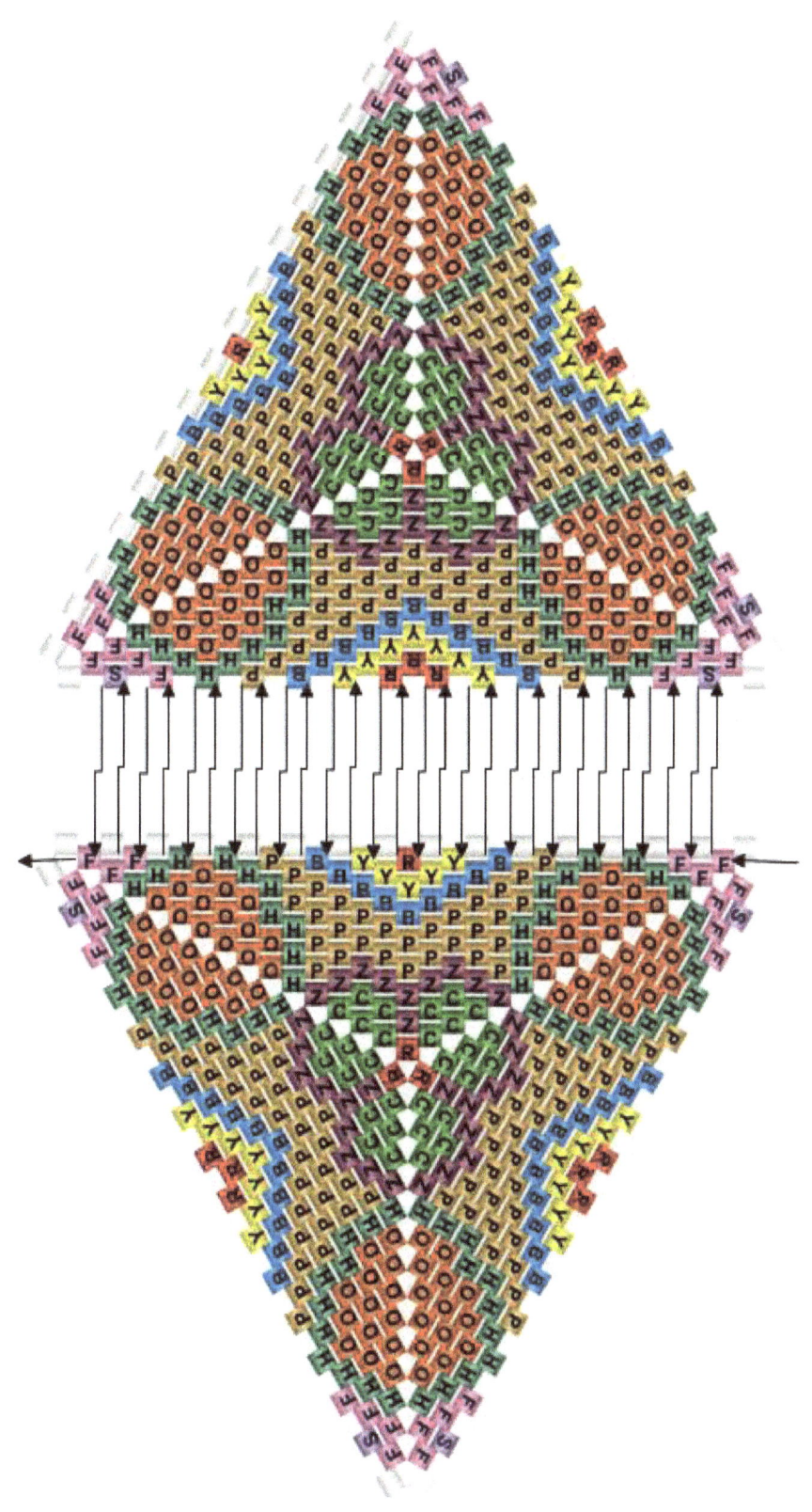

3D Beading Patterns..........79

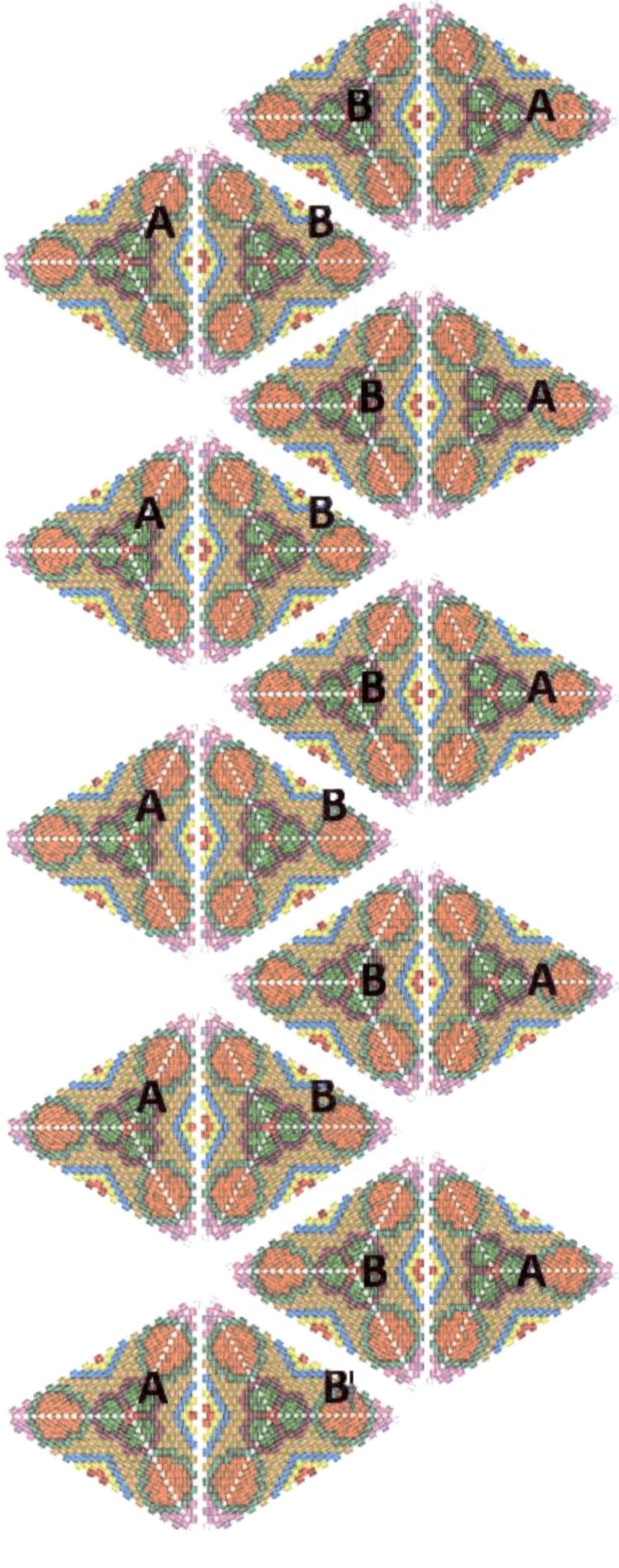

3D Ball – All Piece Demo and Assembling Instruction

Element A:
- 10 pieces
- Please follow Element A instructions to bead. Note each piece has one side with extra row

Element B:
- 10 pieces
- Please follow Element B instructions to bead. Note each piece has two sides with extra row

Assembling:
- Please follow the pattern on the left to sew them together
- Before closing the last piece, fill in the ball with plank foam to keep the ball shape
- After all the 20 triangle pieces are assembled to a ball, sew the 12 mm ball beads to the holes at the joint pointers

80..........April Days

Ice Reflection

BALL DESCRIPTION:

16 rows, approximately the size of soccer ball, made with 20 pieces of triangles

MATERIALS

1. Perler Beads: 7,620 pieces, 9 colors
2. Ball Beads: 12 pieces, 12 mm in diameter, 1 color
3. Beading String: fishing line – 6 lbs. 160 in for one triangle piece and the ball bead
4. Inside filling: used plank foam

TOOLS

1. Needle: size of 2.5 in
2. Curved needle: size of 3.5 in
3. Scissors
4. Stainless steel tweezer

Color and Number of Beads

1) Perler beads:

Symbol ID	Color preview	Count
C		60
L		180
P		1 260
M		1 380
W		960
Y		1 620
G		1 200
O		720
R		240
Skip		~~60~~

2) Ball beads:

Red		12 ball beads (12 mm) – for 12 holes at joint

Note: The colors presented above and on pictures are not precise to show the colors on the actual product.

Element A: Letter Notation

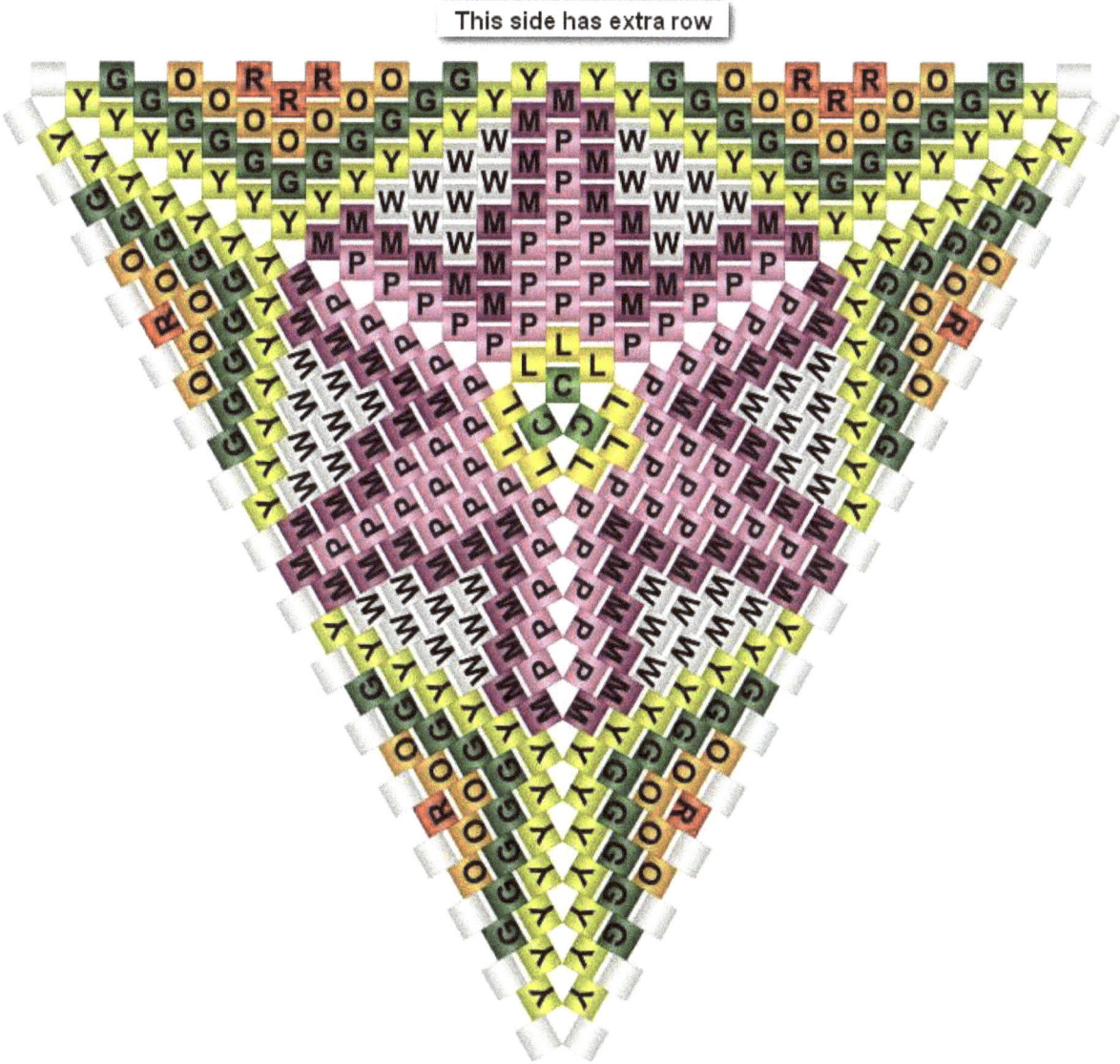

Important: All the white indicators on the graphic are location marking only. There are no beads needed for the places. Please skip all of them by following the element build instruction.

3D Beading Patterns..........83

Element A: Instruction

Total 16 rows

Row 1: 3C.

Row 2: 2L. 2L. 2L.

Row 3: 2P, 1L. 2P, 1L. 2P, 1L.

Row 4: 2P, 1P, 1P. 2P, 1P, 1P. 2P, 1P, 1P.

Row 5: 2P. 1M, 1P, 1M. 2P. 1M, 1P, 1M. 2P. 1M, 1P, 1M.

Row 6: 2P, 1M, 1P, 1P, 1M. 2P, 1M, 1P, 1P, 1M. 2P, 1M, 1P, 1P, 1M.

Row 7: 2P, 1M, 1M, 1P, 1M, 1M. 2P, 1M, 1M, 1P, 1M, 1M. 2P, 1M, 1M, 1P, 1M, 1M.

Row 8: 2M, 1M, 1W, 1P, 1P, 1W, 1M. 2M, 1M, 1W, 1P, 1P, 1W, 1M. 2M, 1M, 1W, 1P, 1P, 1W, 1M.

Row 9: 2Y, 1M, 1W, 1M, 1P, 1M, 1W, 1M. 2Y, 1M, 1W, 1M, 1P, 1M, 1W, 1M.

2Y, 1M, 1W, 1M, 1P, 1M, 1W, 1M.

Row 10: 2Y, 1Y, 1W, 1W, 1M, 1M, 1W, 1W, 1Y. 2Y, 1Y, 1W, 1W, 1M, 1M, 1W, 1W, 1Y.

2Y, 1Y, 1W, 1W, 1M, 1M, 1W, 1W, 1Y.

Row 11: 2Y, 1G, 1Y, 1W, 1W, 1P, 1W, 1W, 1Y, 1G. 2Y, 1G, 1Y, 1W, 1W, 1P, 1W, 1W, 1Y, 1G.

2Y, 1G, 1Y, 1W, 1W, 1P, 1W, 1W, 1Y, 1G.

Row 12: 2Y, 1G, 1G, 1Y, 1W, 1M, 1M, 1W, 1Y, 1G, 1G. 2Y, 1G, 1G, 1Y, 1W, 1M, 1M, 1W, 1Y, 1G, 1G.

2Y, 1G, 1G, 1Y, 1W, 1M, 1M, 1W, 1Y, 1G, 1G.

Row 13: 2Y, 1G, 1O, 1G, 1Y, 1W, 1P, 1W, 1Y, 1G, 1O, 1G.

2Y, 1G, 1O, 1G, 1Y, 1W, 1P, 1W, 1Y, 1G, 1O, 1G.

2Y, 1G, 1O, 1G, 1Y, 1W, 1P, 1W, 1Y, 1G, 1O, 1G.

Row 14: 2Y, 1G, 1O, 1O, 1G, 1Y, 1M 1M, 1Y, 1G, 1O, 1O, 1G.

2Y, 1G, 1O, 1O, 1G, 1Y, 1M 1M, 1Y, 1G, 1O, 1O, 1G.

2Y, 1G, 1O, 1O, 1G, 1Y, 1M 1M, 1Y, 1G, 1O, 1O, 1G.

Row 15: 2Y, 1G, 1O, 1R, 1O, 1G, 1Y, 1M, 1Y, 1G, 1O, 1R, 1O, 1G.

2Y, 1G, 1O, 1R, 1O, 1G, 1Y, 1M, 1Y, 1G, 1O, 1R, 1O, 1G.

2Y, 1G, 1O, 1R, 1O, 1G, 1Y, 1M, 1Y, 1G, 1O, 1R, 1O, 1G.

The following is the extra row:

Row 16: Skip, 1G, 1O, 1R, 1R, 1O, 1G, 1Y, 1Y, 1G, 1O, 1R, 1R, 1O, 1G.

Element A: Number Notation

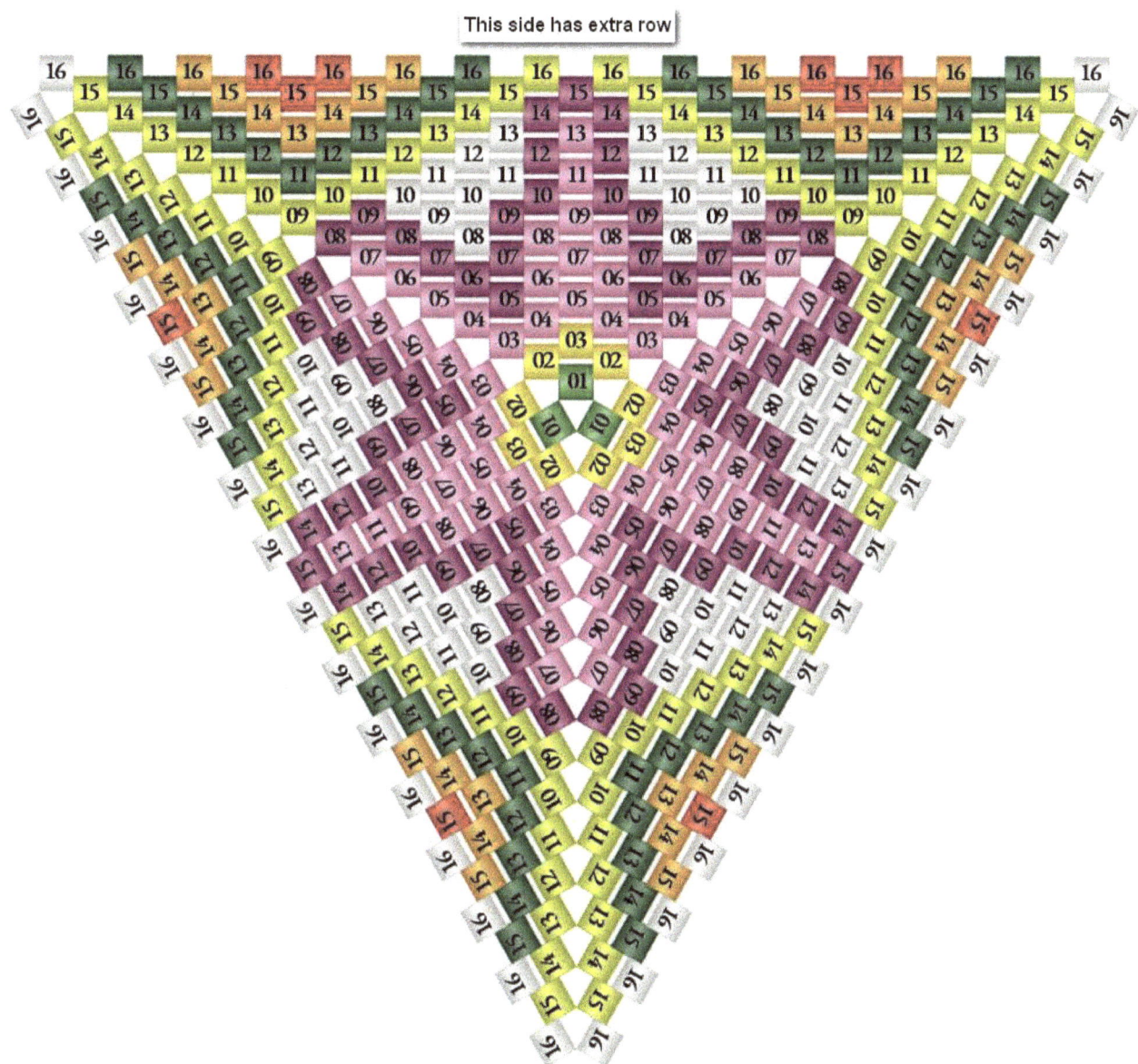

Important: All the white indicators on the graphic are location marking only. There are no beads needed for the places. Please skip all of them by following the element build instruction.

Element B: Letter Notation

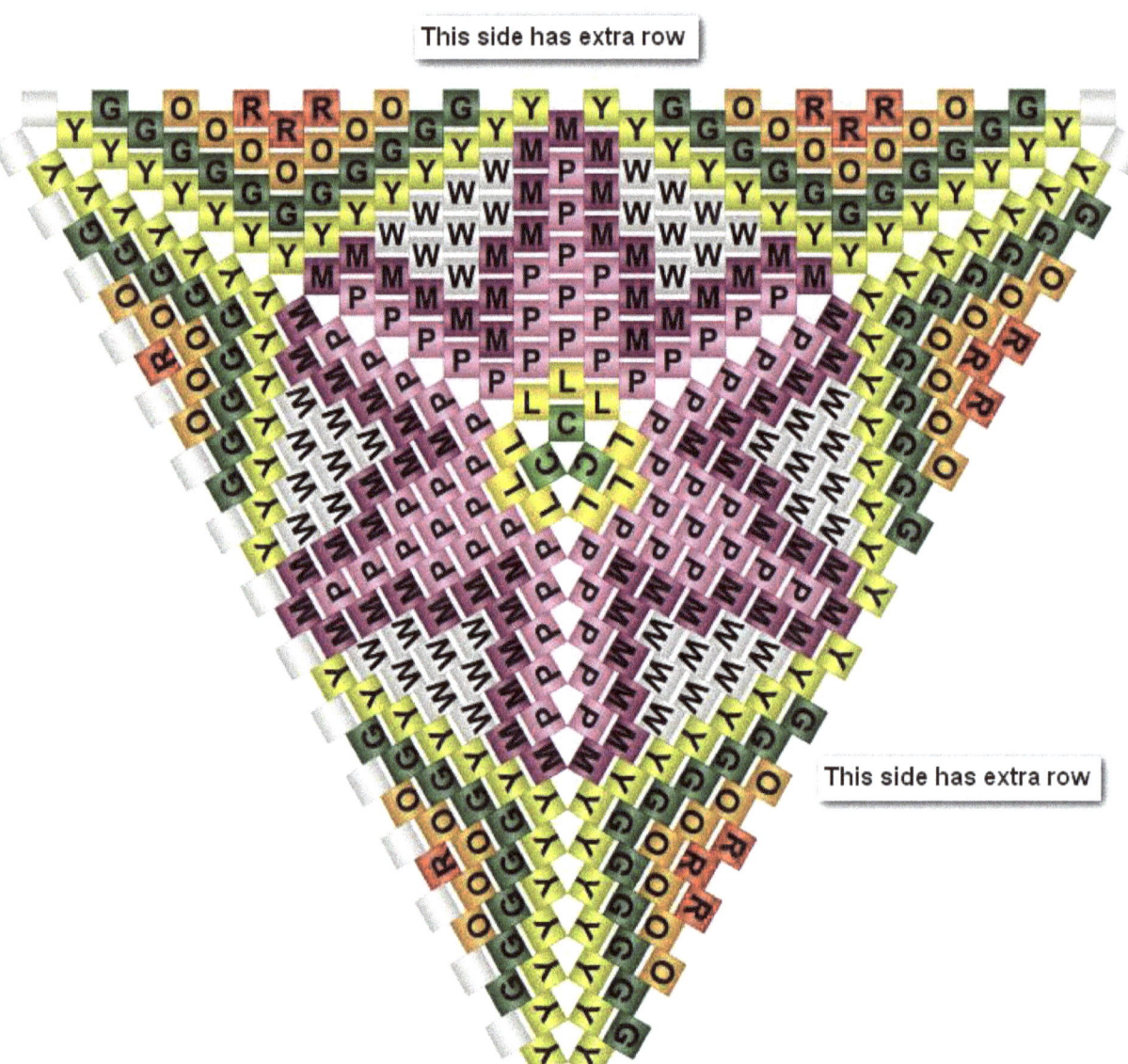

Important: All the white indicators on the graphic are location marking only. There are no beads needed for the places. Please skip all of them by following the element build instruction.

86..........April Days

Element B: Instruction
Total 16 rows

Row 1: 3C.

Row 2: 2L. 2L. 2L.

Row 3: 2P, 1L. 2P, 1L. 2P, 1L.

Row 4: 2P, 1P, 1P. 2P, 1P, 1P. 2P, 1P, 1P.

Row 5: 2P. 1M, 1P, 1M. 2P. 1M, 1P, 1M. 2P. 1M, 1P, 1M.

Row 6: 2P, 1M, 1P, 1P, 1M. 2P, 1M, 1P, 1P, 1M. 2P, 1M, 1P, 1P, 1M.

Row 7: 2P, 1M, 1M, 1P, 1M, 1M. 2P, 1M, 1M, 1P, 1M, 1M. 2P, 1M, 1M, 1P, 1M, 1M.

Row 8: 2M, 1M, 1W, 1P, 1P, 1W, 1M. 2M, 1M, 1W, 1P, 1P, 1W, 1M. 2M, 1M, 1W, 1P, 1P, 1W, 1M.

Row 9: 2Y, 1M, 1W, 1M, 1P, 1M, 1W, 1M. 2Y, 1M, 1W, 1M, 1P, 1M, 1W, 1M.
2Y, 1M, 1W, 1M, 1P, 1M, 1W, 1M.

Row 10: 2Y, 1Y, 1W, 1W, 1M, 1M, 1W, 1W, 1Y. 2Y, 1Y, 1W, 1W, 1M, 1M, 1W, 1W, 1Y.
2Y, 1Y, 1W, 1W, 1M, 1M, 1W, 1W, 1Y.

Row 11: 2Y, 1G, 1Y, 1W, 1W, 1P, 1W, 1W, 1Y, 1G. 2Y, 1G, 1Y, 1W, 1W, 1P, 1W, 1W, 1Y, 1G.
2Y, 1G, 1Y, 1W, 1W, 1P, 1W, 1W, 1Y, 1G.

Row 12: 2Y, 1G, 1G, 1Y, 1W, 1M, 1M, 1W, 1Y, 1G, 1G. 2Y, 1G, 1G, 1Y, 1W, 1M, 1M, 1W, 1Y, 1G, 1G.
2Y, 1G, 1G, 1Y, 1W, 1M, 1M, 1W, 1Y, 1G, 1G.

Row 13: 2Y, 1G, 1O, 1G, 1Y, 1W, 1P, 1W, 1Y, 1G, 1O, 1G.
2Y, 1G, 1O, 1G, 1Y, 1W, 1P, 1W, 1Y, 1G, 1O, 1G.
2Y, 1G, 1O, 1G, 1Y, 1W, 1P, 1W, 1Y, 1G, 1O, 1G.

Row 14: 2Y, 1G, 1O, 1O, 1G, 1Y, 1M 1M, 1Y, 1G, 1O, 1O, 1G.
2Y, 1G, 1O, 1O, 1G, 1Y, 1M 1M, 1Y, 1G, 1O, 1O, 1G.
2Y, 1G, 1O, 1O, 1G, 1Y, 1M 1M, 1Y, 1G, 1O, 1O, 1G.

Row 15: 2Y, 1G, 1O, 1R, 1O, 1G, 1Y, 1M, 1Y, 1G, 1O, 1R, 1O, 1G.
2Y, 1G, 1O, 1R, 1O, 1G, 1Y, 1M, 1Y, 1G, 1O, 1R, 1O, 1G.
2Y, 1G, 1O, 1R, 1O, 1G, 1Y, 1M, 1Y, 1G, 1O, 1R, 1O, 1G.

The following is the extra row:

Row 16: Skip, 1G, 1O, 1R, 1R, 1O, 1G, 1Y, 1Y, 1G, 1O, 1R, 1R, 1O, 1G.
Skip, 1G, 1O, 1R, 1R, 1O, 1G, 1Y, 1Y, 1G, 1O, 1R, 1R, 1O, 1G.

Element B: Number Notation

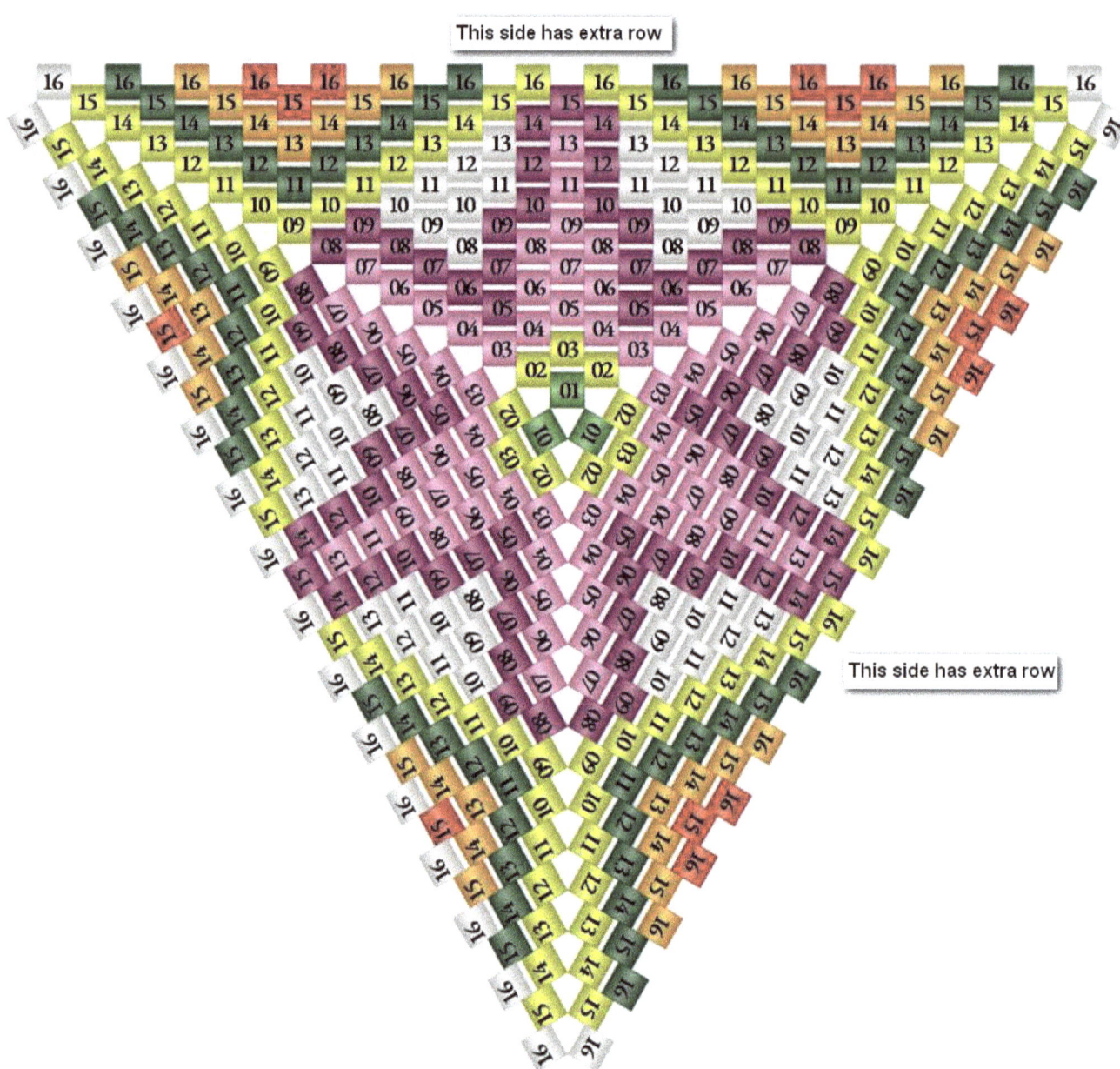

Important: All the white indicators on the graphic are location marking only. There are no beads needed for the places. Please skip all of them by following the element build instruction.

Join Two Triangle Pieces in Zigzag

Note: Please keep the extra string for sewing the ball bead later

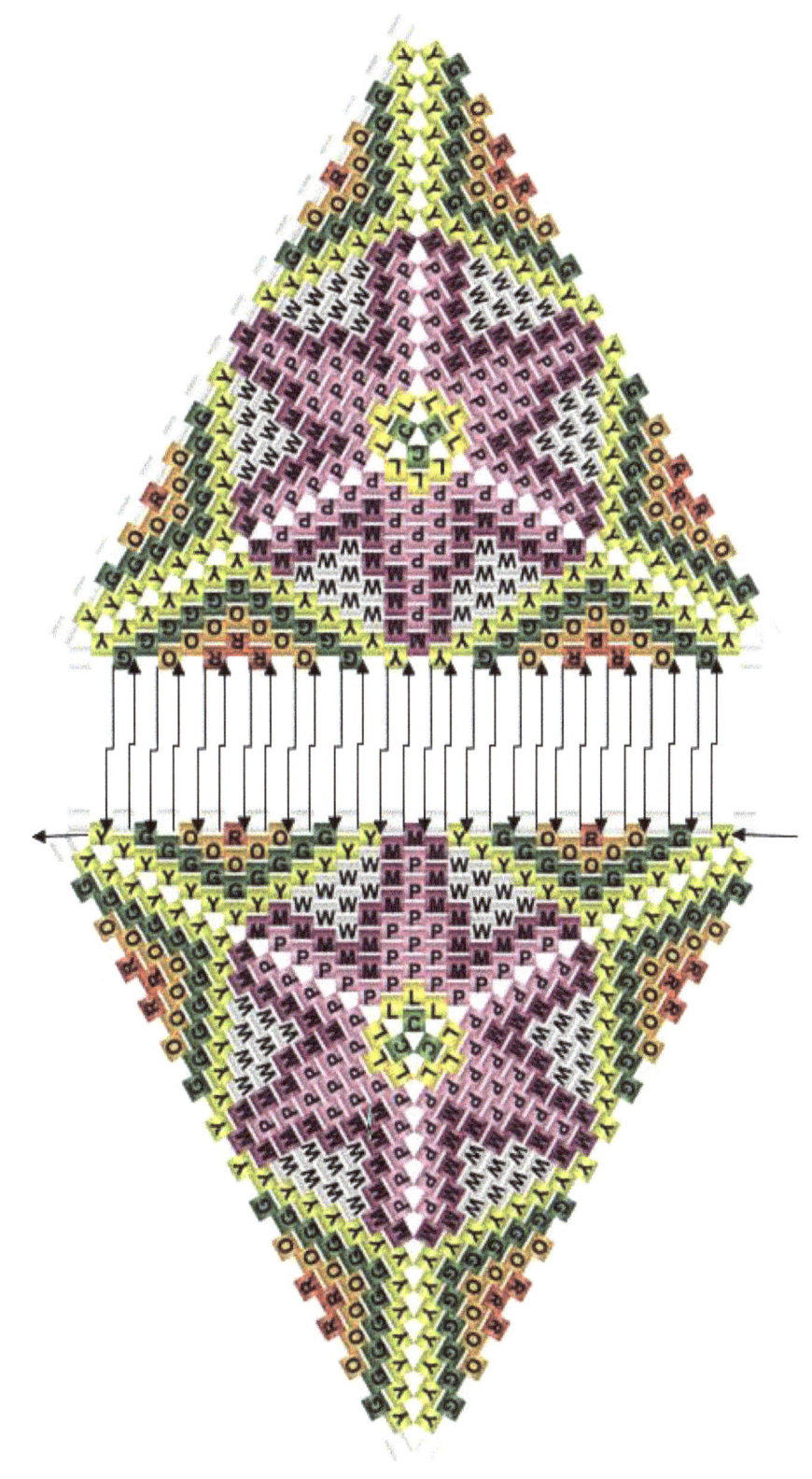

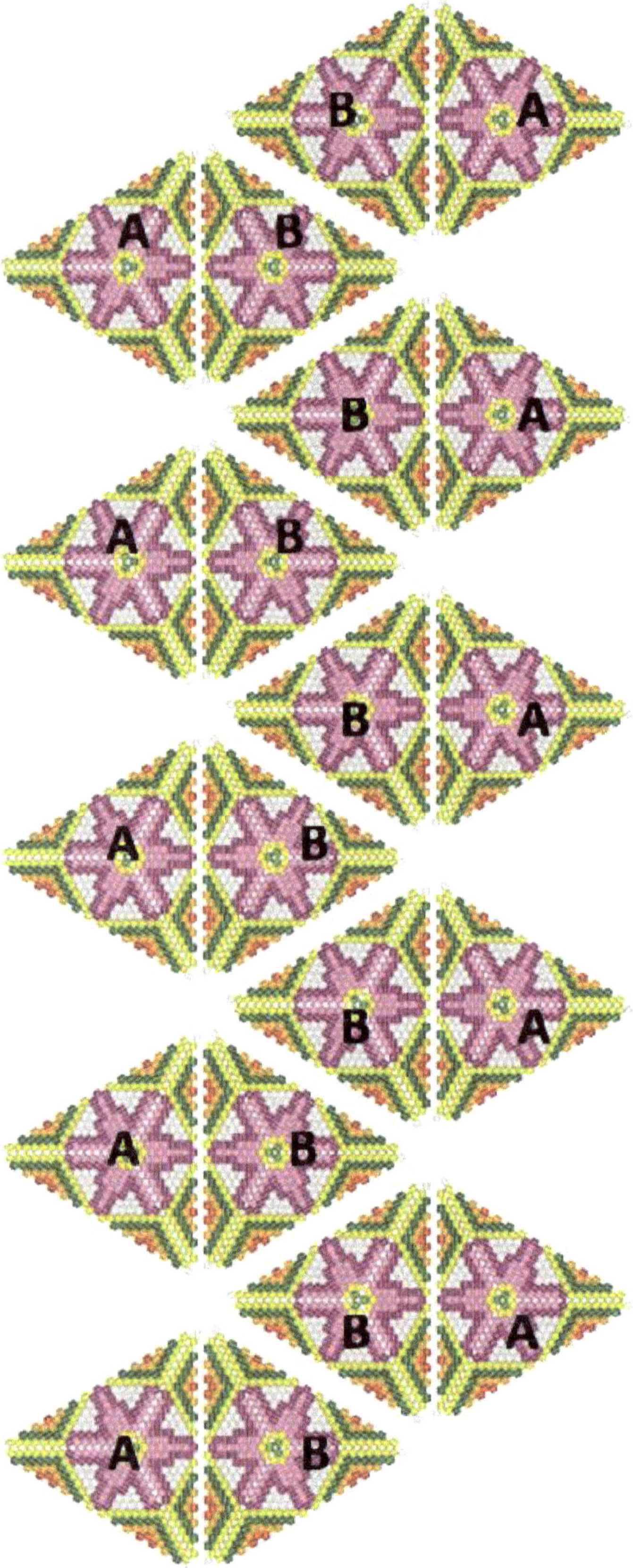

3D Ball – All Piece Demo and Assembling Instruction

Element A:
- 10 pieces
- Please follow Element A instructions to bead. Note each piece has one side with extra row

Element B:
- 10 pieces
- Please follow Element B instructions to bead. Note each piece has two sides with extra row

Assembling:
- Please follow the pattern on the left to sew them together
- Before closing the last piece, fill in the ball with plank foam to keep the ball shape
- After all the 20 triangle pieces are assembled to a ball, sew the 12 mm ball beads to the holes at the joint pointers

Christmas Greeting

BALL DESCRIPTION:

16 rows, approximately the size of soccer ball, made with 20 pieces of triangles

MATERIALS

1. Perler Beads: 7,620 pieces, 7 colors
2. Ball Beads: 12 pieces, 12 mm in diameter, 1 color
3. Beading String: fishing line – 6 lbs. 160 in for one triangle piece and the ball bead
4. Inside filling: used plank foam

TOOLS

1. Needle: size of 2.5 in
2. Curved needle: size of 3.5 in
3. Scissors
4. Stainless steel tweezer

Color and Number of Beads

1) Perler beads:

Symbol ID	Color preview	Count
Z		60
P		1 500
G		2 400
R		1 920
B		1 200
O		480
M		60
Skip		~~60~~

2) Ball beads:

Kiwi lime Green		12 ball beads (12 mm) – for 12 holes at joint

Note: The colors presented above and on pictures are not precise to show the colors on the actual product.

Element A: Letter Notation

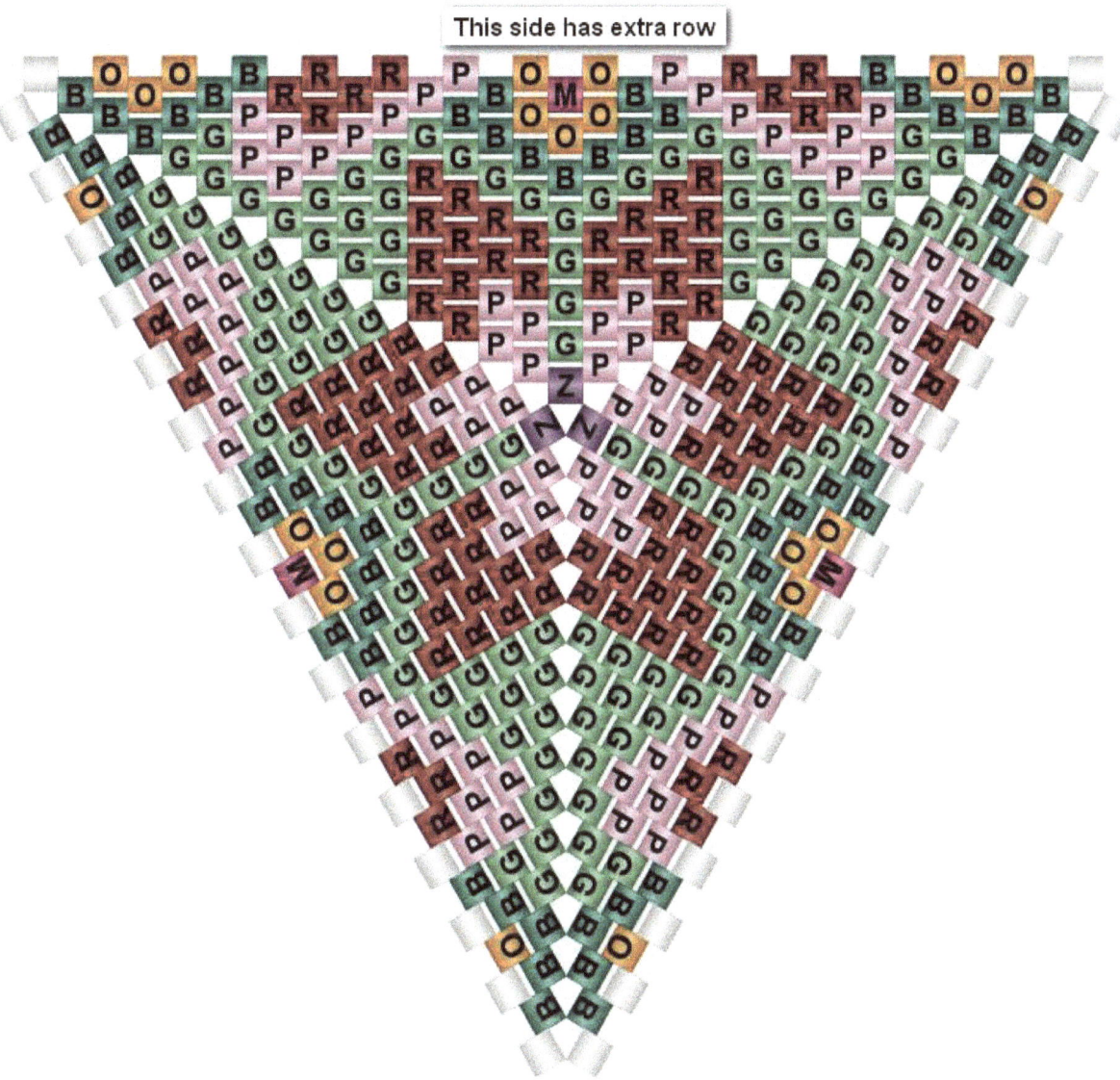

Important: All the white indicators on the graphic are location marking only. There are no beads needed for the places. Please skip all of them by following the element build instruction.

Element A: Instruction

Total 16 rows

Row 1: 3Z

Row 2: 2P, 2P, 2P.

Row 3: 2P, 1G. 2P, 1G. 2P, 1G.

Row 4: 2R, 1P, 1P. 2R, 1P, 1P. 2R, 1P, 1P.

Row 5: 2R, 1P, 1G, 1P. 2R, 1P, 1G, 1P. 2R, 1P, 1G, 1P.

Row 6: 2G, 1R, 1R, 1R, 1R. 2G, 1R, 1R, 1R, 1R. 2G, 1R, 1R, 1R, 1R.

Row 7: 2G, 1R, 1R, 1G, 1R, 1R. 2G, 1R, 1R, 1G, 1R, 1R. 2G, 1R, 1R, 1G, 1R, 1R.

Row 8: 2G, 1G, 1R, 1R, 1R, 1R, 1G. 2G, 1G, 1R, 1R, 1R, 1R, 1G. 2G, 1G, 1R, 1R, 1R, 1R, 1G.

Row 9: 2G,1G,1R,1R,1G,1R,1R,1G. 2G,1G,1R,1R,1G,1R,1R,1G. 2G,1G,1R,1R,1G,1R,1R,1G.

Row 10: 2G, 1G, 1G, 1R, 1G, 1G, 1R, 1G, 1G. 2G, 1G, 1G, 1R, 1G, 1G, 1R, 1G, 1G. 2G, 1G, 1G, 1R, 1G, 1G, 1R, 1G, 1G.

Row 11: 2G, 1P, 1G, 1R, 1G, 1B, 1G, 1R, 1G, 1P. 2G, 1P, 1G, 1R, 1G, 1B, 1G, 1R, 1G, 1P. 2G, 1P, 1G, 1R, 1G, 1B, 1G, 1R, 1G, 1P.

Row 12: 2G, 1P, 1P, 1G, 1G, 1B, 1B, 1G, 1G, 1P, 1P. 2G, 1P, 1P, 1G, 1G, 1B, 1B, 1G, 1G, 1P, 1P. 2G, 1P, 1P, 1G, 1G, 1B, 1B, 1G, 1G, 1P, 1P.

Row 13: 2B, 1G, 1P, 1P, 1G, 1B, 1O, 1B, 1G, 1P, 1P, 1G. 2B, 1G, 1P, 1P, 1G, 1B, 1O, 1B, 1G, 1P, 1P, 1G. 2B, 1G, 1P, 1P, 1G, 1B, 1O, 1B, 1G, 1P, 1P, 1G.

Row 14: 2B, 1B, 1P, 1R, 1P, 1B, 1O, 1O, 1B, 1P, 1R, 1P, 1B. 2B, 1B, 1P, 1R, 1P, 1B, 1O, 1O, 1B, 1P, 1R, 1P, 1B. 2B, 1B, 1P, 1R, 1P, 1B, 1O, 1O, 1B, 1P, 1R, 1P, 1B.

Row 15: 2B, 1O, 1B, 1R, 1R, 1P, 1B, 1M, 1B, 1P, 1R, 1R, 1B, 1O. 2B, 1O, 1B, 1R, 1R, 1P, 1B, 1M, 1B, 1P, 1R, 1R, 1B, 1O. 2B, 1O, 1B, 1R, 1R, 1P, 1B, 1M, 1B, 1P, 1R, 1R, 1B, 1O.

The following is the extra row:

Row 16: Skip, 1O, 1O, 1B, 1R, 1R, 1P, 1O, 1O, 1P, 1R, 1R, 1B, 1O, 1O.

Element A: Number Notation

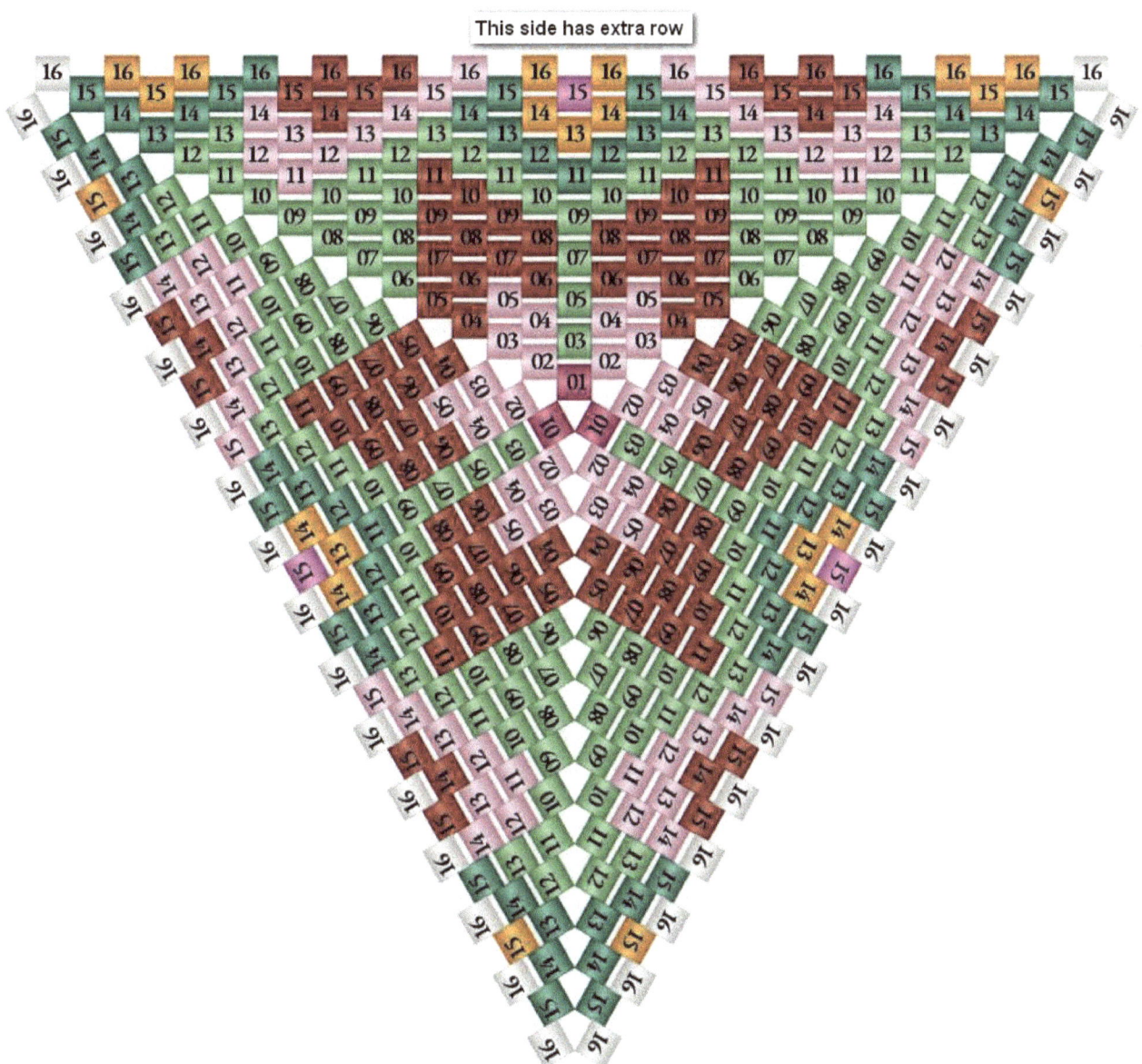

Important: All the white indicators on the graphic are location marking only. There are no beads needed for the places. Please skip all of them by following the element build instruction.

3D Beading Patterns..........95

Element B: Letter Notation

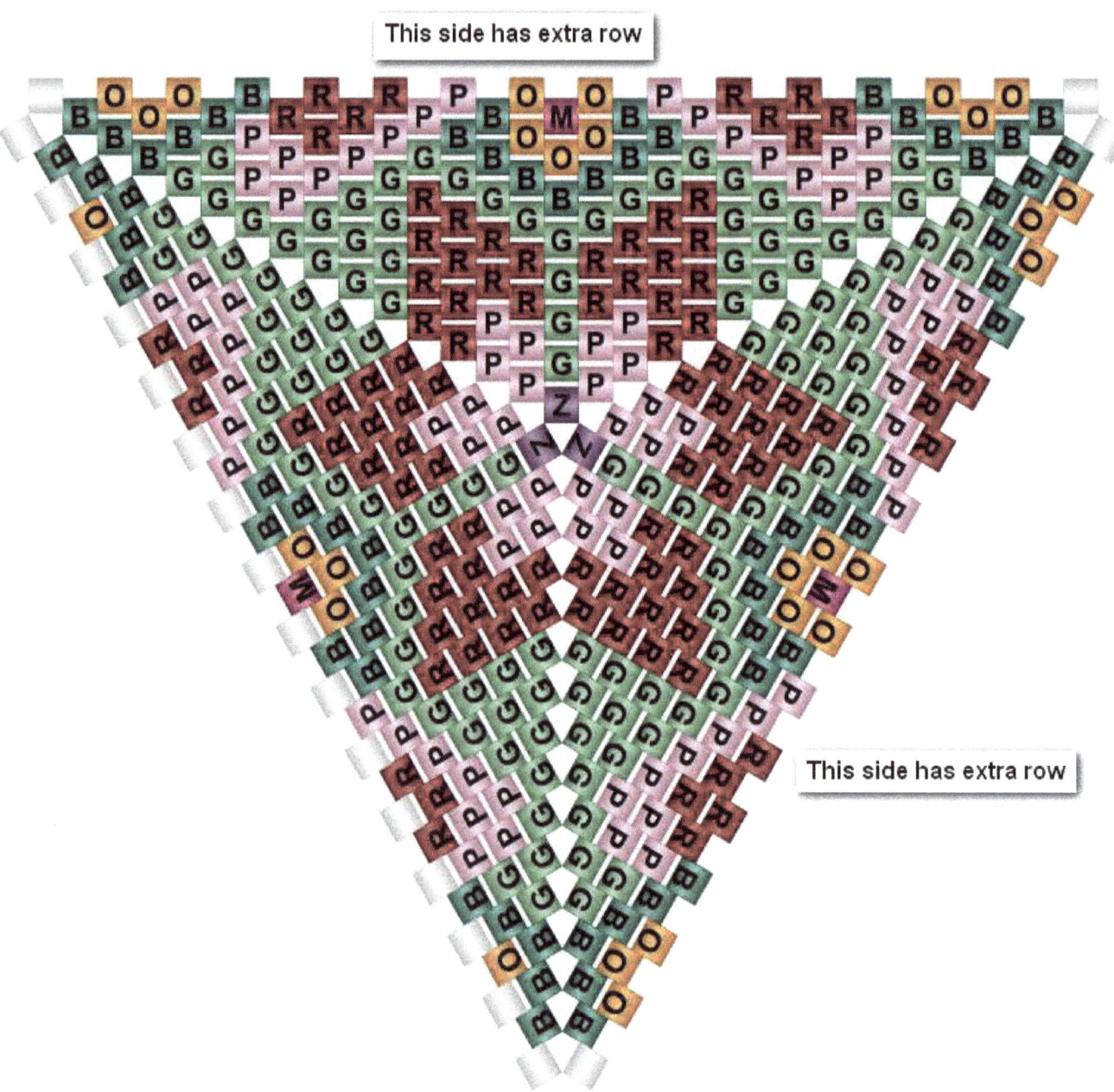

Important: All the white indicators on the graphic are location marking only. There are no beads needed for the places. Please skip all of them by following the element build instruction.

96..........April Days

Element B: Instruction

Total 16 rows

Row 1: 3Z

Row 2: 2P, 2P, 2P.

Row 3: 2P, 1G. 2P, 1G. 2P, 1G.

Row 4: 2R, 1P, 1P. 2R, 1P, 1P. 2R, 1P, 1P.

Row 5: 2R, 1P, 1G, 1P. 2R, 1P, 1G, 1P. 2R, 1P, 1G, 1P.

Row 6: 2G, 1R, 1R, 1R, 1R. 2G, 1R, 1R, 1R, 1R. 2G, 1R, 1R, 1R, 1R.

Row 7: 2G, 1R, 1R, 1G, 1R, 1R. 2G, 1R, 1R, 1G, 1R, 1R. 2G, 1R, 1R, 1G, 1R, 1R.

Row 8: 2G, 1G, 1R, 1R, 1R, 1R, 1G. 2G, 1G, 1R, 1R, 1R, 1R, 1G. 2G, 1G, 1R, 1R, 1R, 1R, 1G.

Row 9: 2G,1G,1R,1R,1G,1R,1R,1G. 2G,1G,1R,1R,1G,1R,1R,1G. 2G,1G,1R,1R,1G,1R,1R,1G.

Row 10: 2G, 1G, 1G, 1R, 1G, 1G, 1R, 1G, 1G. 2G, 1G, 1G, 1R, 1G, 1G, 1R, 1G, 1G.
2G, 1G, 1G, 1R, 1G, 1G, 1R, 1G, 1G.

Row 11: 2G, 1P, 1G, 1R, 1G, 1B, 1G, 1R, 1G, 1P. 2G, 1P, 1G, 1R, 1G, 1B, 1G, 1R, 1G, 1P.
2G, 1P, 1G, 1R, 1G, 1B, 1G, 1R, 1G, 1P.

Row 12: 2G, 1P, 1P, 1G, 1G, 1B, 1B, 1G, 1G, 1P, 1P. 2G, 1P, 1P, 1G, 1G, 1B, 1B, 1G, 1G, 1P, 1P.
2G, 1P, 1P, 1G, 1G, 1B, 1B, 1G, 1G, 1P, 1P.

Row 13: 2B, 1G, 1P, 1P, 1G, 1B, 1O, 1B, 1G, 1P, 1P, 1G. 2B, 1G, 1P, 1P, 1G, 1B, 1O, 1B, 1G, 1P, 1P, 1G.
2B, 1G, 1P, 1P, 1G, 1B, 1O, 1B, 1G, 1P, 1P, 1G.

Row 14: 2B, 1B, 1P, 1R, 1P, 1B, 1O, 1O, 1B, 1P, 1R, 1P, 1B.
2B, 1B, 1P, 1R, 1P, 1B, 1O, 1O, 1B, 1P, 1R, 1P, 1B.
2B, 1B, 1P, 1R, 1P, 1B, 1O, 1O, 1B, 1P, 1R, 1P, 1B.

Row 15: 2B, 1O, 1B, 1R, 1R, 1P, 1B, 1M, 1B, 1P, 1R, 1R, 1B, 1O.
2B, 1O, 1B, 1R, 1R, 1P, 1B, 1M, 1B, 1P, 1R, 1R, 1B, 1O.
2B, 1O, 1B, 1R, 1R, 1P, 1B, 1M, 1B, 1P, 1R, 1R, 1B, 1O.

The following is the extra row:

Row 16: Skip, 1O, 1O, 1B, 1R, 1R, 1P, 1O, 1O, 1P, 1R, 1R, 1B, 1O, 1O.
Skip, 1O, 1O, 1B, 1R, 1R, 1P, 1O, 1O, 1P, 1R, 1R, 1B, 1O, 1O.

Element B: Number Notation

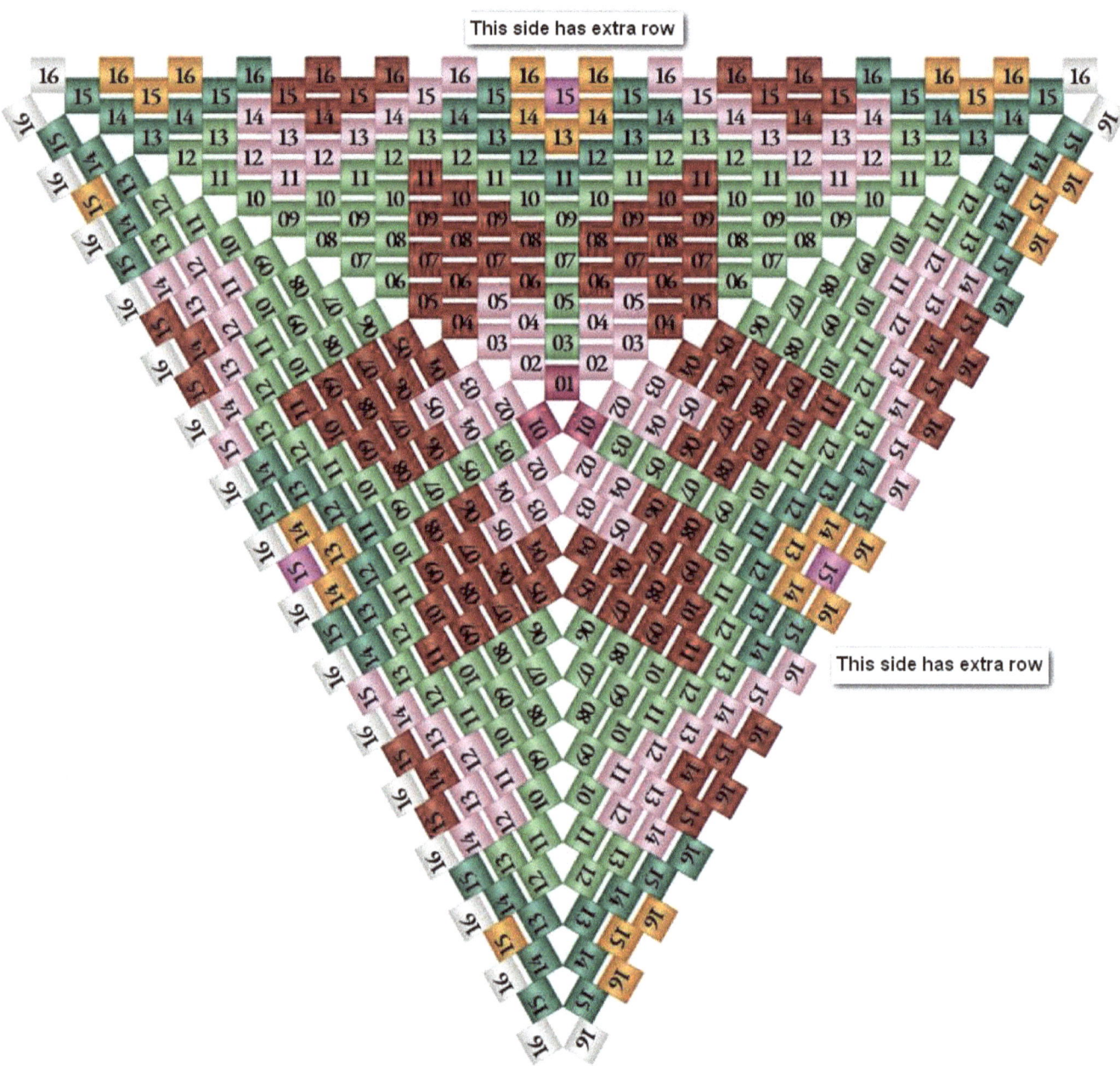

Important: All the white indicators on the graphic are location marking only. There are no beads needed for the places. Please skip all of them by following the element build instruction.

Join Two Triangle Pieces in Zigzag

Note: Please keep the extra string for sewing the ball bead later

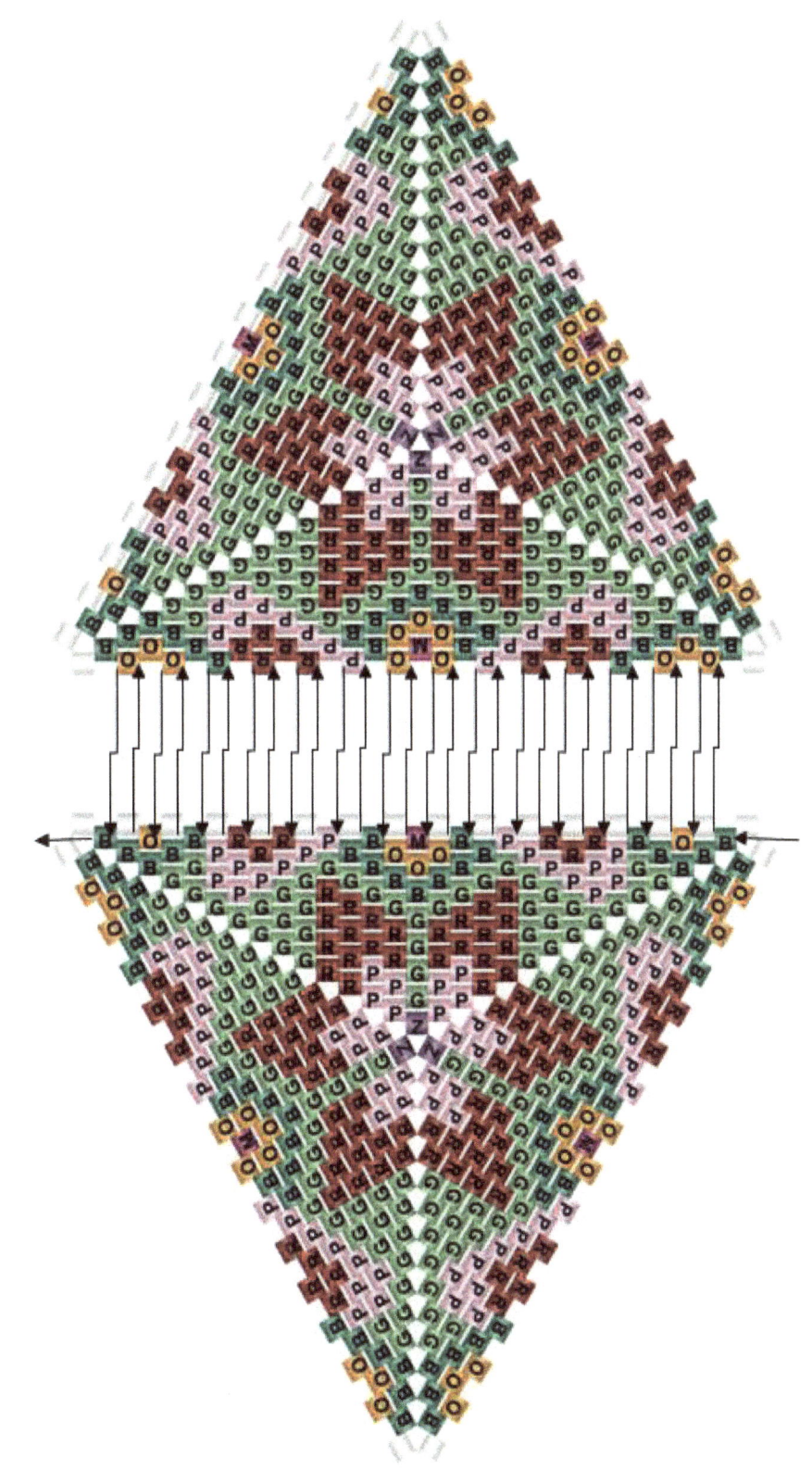

3D Beading Patterns..........99

3D Ball – All Piece Demo and Assembling Instruction

Element A:
- 10 pieces
- Please follow Element A instructions to bead. Note each piece has one side with extra row

Element B:
- 10 pieces
- Please follow Element B instructions to bead. Note each piece has two sides with extra row

Assembling:
- Please follow the pattern on the left to sew them together
- Before closing the last piece, fill in the ball with plank foam to keep the ball shape
- After all the 20 triangle pieces are assembled to a ball, sew the 12 mm ball beads to the holes at the joint pointers

www.ingramcontent.com/pod-product-compliance
Lightning Source LLC
Chambersburg PA
CBHW051317110526
44590CB00031B/4378